In How I Discovered My Mother Was A Goddess, Beverly Charles, tells the poignant story of aging and dementia from the point of view of both the parent and child. At some times troubling and other times darkly comic, it provides a vision of a spiritual journey, one that is healing, authentic, and satisfying. In addition to offering us the story of a mother and daughter as they struggle with old age and death, Beverly moves more deeply into the psyche to understand the goddesses at work in herself and her mother during the various phases of life. We journey through the author's and her mother's relationship to each other and to eight goddesses - Artemis, Hestia, Aphrodite, Athena, Demeter, Persephone, Hera, and Mary. By taking us on this odyssey with her, she not only deepens our understanding of the feminine and the goddesses that personify it, but reveals how these goddesses manifest in everyday life. This story enhances our understanding of the divine feminine. This book is for all those who have loved ones experiencing any form of dementia – as our intellectual connection diminishes, may we become more connected in our hearts. This book is also for women and the men who love them – may we never be ashamed of the journey that brings us home to the goddess within.

# HOW I DISCOVERED MY MOTHER WAS A GODDESS

## A DAUGHTER'S STORY

Beverly Charles

*Beverly Charles*

authorHOUSE®

*AuthorHouse*™
*1663 Liberty Drive*
*Bloomington, IN 47403*
*www.authorhouse.com*
*Phone: 1-800-839-8640*

*First published by AuthorHouse 11/12/2010*

*ISBN: 978-1-4520-9219-5 (sc)*
*ISBN: 978-1-4520-9220-1 (hc)*
*ISBN: 978-1-4520-9221-8 (e)*

*Library of Congress Control Number: 2010915731*

*Printed in the United States of America*

*Certain stock imagery © Thinkstock.*

*This book is printed on acid-free paper.*

# For my mother
# ECSB

For women everywhere –
may we never be ashamed of the journey
that brought us home to our goddess selves.

For all men and women who have loved ones
experiencing any form of dementia –
as our intellectual connection diminishes,
may we become more connected in our hearts.

*"Behind naming, beneath words, is something else.*
*An existence named unnamed and unnameable."*
from "Naming" from Woman and Nature, Susan Griffin

"Writing can be part of the healing process,
taking all our disparate parts into our arms.
We meet ourselves and close a yawning gap....
Knowing this wholeness, the world becomes whole.
No inside, no outside. No here and no there.
No one too foreign or difficult not to be embraced."
- from *The Great Failure*, Natalie Goldberg

# AUTHOR'S NOTE

Memoir is a form of creative non-fiction, and the word is joined in the thesaurus by these words – life-story, autobiography, diary, reminiscences, recollections, journal, chronicle, and history. I have used most of these forms in writing my own memoir.

My life has been experienced in numerous communities – family of origin, extended family, friends, churches, schools, marriages, children, grandchildren, work, hospitals, nursing homes, cities, towns, villages, the south, the mid-west, the west, abroad,.....The stories that come together to make this book, *How I Discovered My Mother Was A Goddess*, are influenced by that life experience. I have recreated all conversations and events as accurately as I could. Someone else might tell the story differently, but this is how I experienced it. It's my story.

I have changed some of the names in the story, and I have received permission from the individuals whose names are not changed. I am grateful to all who lived this story with me.

> *"One cannot and must not try to erase the past*
> *merely because it does not fit the present."*
> *- Golda Meir, former Prime Minister of Israel*

# CONTENTS

# INTRODUCTION

## DEMENTIA

## THE JOURNEY

*"Let compassion breathe in and out of you, filling you and singing."*
– from *Waiting*, Jane Cooper, poet essayist, teacher, Guggenheim Fellow

# Introduction

My mother was diagnosed with senile dementia in 2003. Since then, I have observed her regress from aging adult to young adult, adolescent to pre-adolescent, child to toddler, and infant to ghost in a body. As we take this journey together, she sleeps more and more, and I am awakening more and more - to her essence - pure love.

Years earlier, at the onset of her illness, I was given a booklet, *Finding the Answers: A Resource Guide for Caregivers*. Opening it, I read: This guide consists of three parts…practical advice on all aspects of caring for someone with Alzheimer's disease…specific suggestions for handling everyday concerns…a comprehensive list of resources and organizations that may be helpful to you.

The booklet was helpful, but it did not tell me what I had to discover on my own. My book, *How I Discovered My Mother Was A Goddess*, is a daughter's story, one that contains what the Alzheimers guidebook did not, a roadmap of the journey I would take with my mother, offering a time of remembering, facing up to, sitting in silence with, and discovering a stillness where only love abides. It has been a time to reconcile what we share – our feminine being. We are girls, women, females, girlfriends, lovers, wives, sisters, mothers, aunts, grandmothers, crones, goddesses…. For five years I have been sitting with my mother, remembering for her, for us, trying to memorize her in preparation for the time when I will no longer have her with me…. Recently, as I walked on the beach in Port Aransas where I live, I stopped to observe a local marine scientist put on his rubber gloves and begin to examine a dead Kemp's Ridley Turtle.

"What happened?" I inquired.

"Her side was sheared off by a boat propeller."

"Was she coming ashore to nest?"

"It's the nesting season."

He loaded her into his truck bed and drove off.

I had been writing a piece about mother and her senile dementia titled "Heart-Breaker" when I came upon the scientist and the dead turtle. I went home and Googled Kemp's Ridley Turtles. I found that they are an endangered species and will struggle to the point of death if captured. Fishermen in times past believed that the Kemp's Ridley Turtle would die of a broken heart if laid on its back on a ship deck, so it came to be known as the heart-break turtle. I decided the Kemp's Ridley and my mother had something in common. They were both endangered species, they both had the will to struggle to the point of death, and they both would die of a broken heart if confined.

In Native American cultures and in Southern Asia, the turtle has profound symbolism and is believed to carry the world, or to represent the cosmos, its upper shell being the heavens, its body the earth, and its undershell the water or underworld. A creature of both water and land, the turtle generally represents femininity.

The Kemp's Ridley and my mother have something else in common. They had eggs that were intended to give life. If effectively fertilized and incubated, they produce more of the species from which they came. What a symbol of hope – to give life to more of the same.

The paradox of birth, though, is that it also delivers death. The power of the mother brings one into relationship with both life and death. The turtle eggs, carried inside a swimming, intentional mother, are headed for a spot on a sandy beach where the mother will make a nest for them. Hundreds of baby turtles will work, against all odds, to make it from that nest to the sea to grow and create more of the same. Likewise, the human egg nests in the womb for nine months, curled up, warm, growing, only to be thrust out into the world at the end of its incubation to make it from the womb to the tomb with some measure of meaning.

What does it mean to *mother?* To *be mothered?* Now I have become my mother's mother. Because at my mother's care facility there are so few staff and so many elderly to feed, I arrange my visits for mealtime. Now I feed her with a spoon and wipe the dribble from her chin. Sometimes she opens her eyes, but mostly she lies back in her geriatric chair waiting for the next bite. I wonder how someone knows to swallow when, for all practical purposes, she is asleep. I imagine how my mother must have fed me as an infant. She would have talked to me.

"Mom, this is one of your favorites, peaches," I say as I spoon them into her open mouth. "Yummy, huh?"

When I press the five keys with the code to let me out of the secured unit, I think how technology and modern medicine have given us the power to hold onto life, or at least to the body that we often associate with life. I compare my mother's artificial world with the natural world of flowering plants, rivers, and animals that she loved. I wonder if her soul is imprisoned in her body. If life and death are natural processes, why do we resist death?

Is this mother I feed now truly my mother? Webster defines mother as the *origin of anything; native; original*. My mother represents my origin. She gave birth to me. I am her daughter. If Jesus is the Son of God, who is the daughter of God? If the Father is God, is the Mother, Mary, a Goddess? If the Holy Spirit abides in us all, what is the vessel, the container that embraces this spirit? My mother is dying – did she matter? Do I matter?

These are the questions simmering when I think of how I discovered my mother was a goddess. A friend asked me, "What is a goddess?" I went to three thesauruses and not one had the word goddess in it. Then I went to my own study where there were two shelves of goddess books. I realized as I pulled out books written and read in the last thirty-five years that I have been trying to define that for a long time.

Being with my mother these past five years has given me the opportunity to discover what she had been demonstrating to me for a lifetime. Now I am taking the time to notice the feminine blessings of the goddesses that dwell within my mother, and within us all.

# CHAPTER ONE

## THE DOOR WAS OPEN

## ARTEMIS

## GODDESS OF WILDLIFE AND INDEPENDENT FEMININE SPIRIT

*"I am an honest woman: I earn my living.*
*I am a free woman: I live in my own house...."*
– Lina in George Bernard Shaw's Misalliance

The Beginning

# The Door Was Open

"Mother," I call at her open back door.

I have just driven one hundred and forty miles over familiar Texas back roads. Growing up, I lived in many of the little towns on this familiar stretch that now brings me from my island home to the rural town where seven generations of my maternal family have lived. My mother left at twenty-two and returned at age seventy-seven, here, to Hallettsville.

But why is the door unlocked? My mother, a widow for twenty-seven years, has always locked doors and windows, and if she was feeling particularly fearful, she moved tables and chairs in front of them. My hand perspires on the doorknob. I pause, remembering to breathe. I wonder what awaits me inside.

She had been complaining for months about her health and lack of help to do the yard. She'd sworn, after years of moving around with my father, who I'd always called Daddy, that she'd never move again. But now, like her middle-child brother, Howard, she had returned. Her oldest brother, Curtis, a dairy farmer, had never left. I have to admit, I found the idea of this move comforting. She enjoyed the company of her brothers and her sisters-in-law, and the town was small and manageable by car and on foot.

Now I stand in her open back door. The apartment-sized electric stove faces me. She has printed on lined paper – *DO NOT LEAVE BURNERS ON* – and taped it above the range. My eyes move to the full-sized refrigerator. It is covered with family pictures held to its surface by magnets she has collected through the years. In one of them, my Aunt Sis, recently deceased, stares at me from a rocking chair. Her image is held up by a quilted magnet, edged in eyelet, embroidered with the message, *A friend is a gift you give yourself.* I step inside. The smell of coffee lingers in the air. It is ten-thirty in the morning. I check the electric pot and it is still on. I flip the switch to off. That coffee is thick, I think, if she got up at her usual five a.m.

I move past the refrigerator into the archway that divides the dining area from the living room, where she is huddled, shrinking in her big sky blue velour tufted rocker. *Is she breathing?*

"Mother," I say, trying to mask the panic in my voice, "Mother?"

Her big blue eyes are open but they don't see me. Her short, stunningly white hair hasn't been brushed. I notice she needs a haircut. She has always worn it short. My daddy cut it when he was still alive, and she cut it herself until the last year. My mother, who is always up, dressed in her skirt or slacks, blouse, earbobs, and makeup by seven a.m., is sitting here in her purple fleece robe and slippers at ten-thirty in the morning. The house is an oven. I check the thermostat. The heat is on, in spite of the ninety-plus degree temperature on this July morning in Texas. With her eyesight failing, she had recently put a dot of red nail polish on the heat indicator so she could tell the difference in the heat and cool settings. I turn the thermostat to cool, adjust the temperature, close the front and back doors, and turn on a fan.

Kneeling beside her, I ask, "Are you okay, Mother?"

My throat tightens.

For the first time since I arrived, she speaks. "You need to get the birds out of my bedroom. They came in all night through that window by my dresser."

"Mother," I say.

"Go see for yourself," she commands. I have either been following or resisting her commands for as long as I can remember.

Walking to the bedroom with her behind me, I look at the closed, shaded, curtained window. It has not been opened in years. I pull back the curtain and shade to discover that she has nailed it shut at some point.

"Mother, there are no birds here," I assure her.

"I know they were here. There were three ragamuffins here too."

I listen, wondering what to say or do.

"Did you hear me? There were three of them, two girls and a boy."

"What did they want?" I ask.

"They looked hungry. I offered them supper but they wouldn't eat."

I imagine my mother, a really good cook, offering up her beefy meatloaf, full of onions and spices and a dash of Worcestershire Sauce, topped with ketchup, hot from the oven. Maybe she served it with her homemade mashed potatoes, rich with butter, stirred up with lots of salt and pepper. Did she also have boiled cabbage served with a splash of homemade chile patine pepper sauce? And there would be a green salad and hot cornbread. All the food groups. How dare those ragamuffins refuse my mother's home cooked feast!

"Birds," she says.

Of course, she sees birds. The wallpaper above the chair rail in her bedroom had birds on it – cardinals, bluebirds, goldfinches. I had thought we'd change it when she moved in, but she liked it.

"I love birds," she'd said.

So I had given the beaded ceiling a fresh coat of white paint and covered the brown paneling below the chair rail with the same white to brighten the room.

I pick up, off her dresser, a porcelain powder dish and a little flowered poodle figurine, remembering the day my brother, Bobby, and I went to Perry Brothers with our pockets full of nickels and dimes and bought them for her.

"This furniture is fifty-three years old," I hear myself saying aloud.

"And it's still good," she replies. "They used to make things to last."

I raise my head, looking upward, beseeching.

"Look under the bed. They hide there," she tells me.

I don't argue with her. I get on my knees, lift the dust ruffle and say, "no sign of them here." This is not the double bed we moved in here five years ago. She wanted more space in her room and asked me to find her a single bed. I did. From double bed to single bed, from larger house to smaller house, from flower beds to flower pots – her life is shrinking before my eyes.

"I know they're hiding there. Tell them to leave."

"I will."

I reach for the phone on the shelf in the living room corner and dial her doctor's number. I have it memorized after five years of accompanying her to her regular appointments. I recall him telling us several years before that her MRI revealed her brain looked like the state of Minnesota, land of many lakes, because she'd had so many mini-strokes. She had laughed and told that story to everyone. My Aunt Dot said, "I don't think that's very funny." Later, my mother said, "Dot needs a sense of humor."

As I look at her now, I wonder if she has had another TIA, transient ischemic attack. That's what the doctor labeled them.

When the receptionist answers, she reports that Dr. Robinson is out of town for the weekend and says, "I can make you an appointment for Monday morning. If it's an emergency, I'll contact the doctor on call."

I had come this morning to pick up my mother to take her home with me for the Fourth of July weekend, thinking about it with fond memories. She had always loved this holiday and would regale us with stories of celebrations when she was a girl – "parades, picnics, firecrackers, political speeches, tablecloths on the ground, and picnic baskets." She enjoyed sitting on our deck in Port Aransas and watching the fireworks display light up the night sky. She would buy sparklers for her children, grandchildren, and great-grandchildren. She'd stir up mountains of mustardy, dilly potato salad, fry lots of chicken, bake a ham (to accommodate my non-fowl eating habit), and assume we'd eat outdoors. Flies, heat, and mosquitoes never kept us from enjoying a picnic.

I hug her to me, remembering her passion for life.

To the receptionist, I say, "It's not an emergency. I'm taking her home with me. Happy Fourth of July. See you on Monday at 10:30."

"Momma," I say, "let's find you something to wear."

A red, white, and blue scarf dangling from a pegged hanger on the back of the door catches my eye. I'd seen that same scarf wrapped above the brim of a white straw hat she often wore.

"Do you want to wear red, white, and blue?" I inquire. "It's almost the Fourth of July."

Something shifts. She takes the scarf from my hand, pulls her white hat from the shelf, and wraps the scarf around it the same way I've seen her do many times before. She puts on navy slacks and a white blouse. Then earbobs.

I help her pack. It is slow. I feel my impatience returning. I am hurrying her.

She says, "Don't rush me."

I suddenly realize I don't even know what time it is. Noon. It is almost noon. This hour and a half has seemed like an eternity. I call my husband, Larry, telling him we are stopping for lunch, "We should be there around four."

I take my mother's hand in one of mine, her suitcase in the other, lock her house and we move slowly toward my silver Ford Taurus at the back of her house.

"Do you have a new car?" she asks.

She has made many trips in this car. I stifle my impulse to tell her it is, and just say, "No."

I buckle her into the passenger side, close the door, and walk around to the driver's side. I stand under a giant Liveoak. I breathe in the musty, loamy smell that takes me three blocks away to what was once my grandmother's house, my mother's mother's house. My roots here are as deep as these live oak roots. How do you take flight with such deep roots, I wonder.

When I open my car door, I am greeted with a frantic demand. "Put the ragamuffins out. They're in the back seat. I don't want them to go with us."

I turn and look in the back seat, saying, "I think they heard you and left." It appears to satisfy her.

We drive through at the local Dairy Queen and take our food to the park to eat. Outside, even in the heat, I feel us both relax as we picnic here in view of the house where we celebrated her seventieth birthday with a grand party.

My mother tells me, pointing, "Miz Hope Finkelstein willed that house and this land to the city for a park. Miz Hope loved your Uncle Curtis. He always mowed for her and checked in on her."

I have heard this story almost every time we picnic in this park, but I still love to hear it. I feel connected to her by her stories.

We toss our trash in the barrel as we walk toward the car. I am behind her. She moves with confidence now, as she always has, in spite of her arthritic, bunioned feet. She is energized by this time out-of-doors. She picks up her pace, turns to me saying, "Why are you lagging behind?"

I want this mother of mine to stay here with me. I know her better.

In the car, she chatters and dozes. Once, upon awaking, she asks, "Are those ragamuffins still in the back seat?"

\* \* \*

Throughout the weekend at our house, she worries about the

presence of the three children. "Why won't they leave me alone? Can't you see the teenaged girl and the little boy and girl with her?"

The first evening as she prepares for bed, she yells, "Larry, Larry, those kids are under my bed. Get them out!"

The following night, at dinner, she has difficulty cutting her meat. I find myself standing beside her, knife in hand, carving her meat into bite-sized pieces as she had so often done for me as a child. Tears burn, wanting to be released. Could I dare show her my fear and sadness in the face of her debilitated condition?

On our polished pine floors, the sturdy step I had seen in the park has been replaced with a shuffle. She moves slowly down the hall to the bathroom and falls twice. Larry and I pick her up and ask her to let us help her move from room to room. She ignores our requests and falls a third time.

On Sunday, my cousin, Molly, surprises me with a call, saying, "I just wanted to check on Aunt Charlyne."

"That's nice," I reply. "Do you want to talk with her? She's taking a nap, but I can wake her." I picture Molly sitting on her beautiful flagstone patio surrounded by the ferns and flowers she so carefully tends.

"No. I just wanted to make sure she was fine after that emergency room visit last week."

"Emergency room visit?" Now I am hooked. "What emergency room visit?"

"Aunt Charlyne called me to take her to the emergency room last Sunday morning, She thought she was having a heart attack, but it was anxiety," Molly says. "She said you were out-of-state and couldn't be reached. It wasn't her first visit. She'd called her mail lady to take her in a few days before she called for my help."

Guilt and anger stew inside me. Defending myself, I say, "I was out-of-state for a brief work trip, but I never leave without her having my home, office, and cell numbers to call." Thinking of my brother, I quickly add, "Why didn't she call Bobby?" He lives less than an hour away. I feel my defensiveness, the familiar *you aren't tending to things* voice in my head. *I still have a consulting business.. I still work for a living* I console myself.

That voice is interrupted by Molly saying, "Oh, don't worry about it. I didn't mind taking her."

Though I know Molly means what she says, I respond, saying, "She's not your responsibility. I'm sorry."

We chat for a few minutes about our holiday weekend and I hang up.

*Thank goodness, my mother just went in to take a nap. I don't want to see her right now.*

I find Larry on the deck. He's reading Larry McMurtry's *Duane's Depressed*, taking advantage of his time alone outdoors to smoke a cigarette. He snuffs out the cigarette, motioning me toward the white Adirondack chair across from him. Sabal Palms we planted for the births of each of our grandchildren, the death of a dear friend, and Larry's retirement after thirty-three years as a school principal tower above us. The roar of the Gulf of Mexico at the end of our street sets the mood for our conversation.

"Can you believe it? Mother admitted herself to the emergency room twice in the last two weeks. Both times she said she was having a heart attack and both times she was diagnosed with acute anxiety."

"How'd you find out about that?" he asks.

"Molly just called and told me." I feel wild with my own assumed motivations and accusations. "Mother wants everyone to think I'm a horrible, irresponsible daughter," I shout.

"She can be manipulative alright," he replies.

"Don't call my mother names," I cry, literally bursting into tears.

Larry strides from the deck. I am left alone with my failure – *I am a selfish daughter.* It's a mantra that rings in my ears. I cannot shut it up. I want to run away and sit alone under a tree in the woods. Artemis, the goddess not defined by relationships, calls to me. She personifies what it means to have an intense reaction, take a stand, rush headlong into things, and step in to assist others. Artemis also reminds me of the unanticipated aspects and results of my actions. Like Artemis, I must turn inward to reflect on what is important to me. I put on my Tevas and head to the beach for a long walk. When I reach the water's edge, I remove my shoes and feel myself relax as the sand and surf caress my feet. This mother of all mothers, the Gulf of Mexico, is holding me. I stomp along singing a Native American chant to celebrate the earth – *"Mother I feel you under my feet. Mother, I hear your heart beat..."*

I return home an hour later, calling for Larry. We head to the Adirondacks on the deck. "I'm sorry," I offer.

"Me, too," he says.

"This is so hard. I want to be there for her and I don't know how to do it."

"You're trying to be rational with an irrational person."

"Can you believe she got herself to the emergency room *twice*? That's quite a feat, considering she has no car."

I had heard stories from friends about a parent's resistance to giving up their last symbol of independence, their automobile, which could have prepared me for this now. But my experience had been different.

Four years earlier, my mother told me – "Sell my car. I'm afraid to drive."

My suspicions of her motivation delayed my taking action on her request. I'd returned home and told Larry, "I know why she wants me to sell her car. She wants me to drive her everywhere, be with her every moment."

And why wouldn't I have thought so? This mother is in such contrast to the one who, in 1950, told Daddy, "Women have rights, too," as my brother and I stood by our 1941 Chevy and she proclaimed to him that if he didn't teach her to drive, she would get in that car with Bobby and me and teach herself. Daddy taught her. She was the one who taught me to drive a stick shift at age fifteen, too, wanting to ensure that I was never dependent on someone to take me places, even as she took deep breaths and shivered when I came near the side of a bridge or the shoulder of the road.

"You won't have to ask for a ride," she had said, setting her hands on her hips. "You'll be independent."

Her words, "You'll be independent," ring in my ears. For years, I heard them morning, noon, and night, even as I longed for a relationship to lean into, one in which I could relax and give up having to prove just how independent I was. I imagine she had lullabied me to sleep with, "*Rock-a-bye baby, in the treetops, when the wind blows, the cradle will rock, when the bough breaks the cradle will fall, pick yourself up and …*"

In our relationship, Artemis, the independent goddess, was alive and well. The ancient Greeks described Artemis, Athena, and Hestia as virgin goddesses because of their capacity for self-containment and self-reliance. Even though Artemis maintained her self-reliance, she was the one goddess who came to the aid of her mother, Leto.

Once again, I had been called to the aid of my mother. And even then, by the time she asked me to sell her car, I'd already felt the weight of her on me. I had, at her request, been taking care of her finances. She didn't want to write checks or balance her checkbook with her bank statement. She pulled out a plastic file box one afternoon, showing me her durable power of attorney, medical power of attorney, and her will. She informed me I was her designated executor and had power of attorney. She also had copies of the living will she had made at the same time Larry and I had ours done.

I remembered being angry at her that day.

"I went through all the letters and cards and papers I'd saved through the years," she told me. "I destroyed the ones I didn't want anyone to find."

It felt like a personal affront, given all the questions I'd asked her through the years about her life, none of which she'd answered. She told historical family anecdotes and other people's "secrets," but clammed up when asked personal questions about herself. Intrigued by my mother's life before, beyond, and away from me, I felt anger and disappointment that I would not be privy to those parts of her. I had looked for explanations to enhance my understanding of our relationship but she would remain an enigma with missing parts in this puzzle I called Momma or Mother depending on our relationship at the moment.

But about the car, I had been surprised to find she had made a verbal commitment to sell her Ford Escort station wagon to her brother, Howard.

"Beverly Ann, your momma wants to sell me her car. How much do you want for it?" he'd said, calling me out of nowhere.

Familiar irritation stirred in my gut. "She *what?*"

"She wants me to buy her car. She says she's never driving it again. How much do you want for it?" I could hear the pique in his voice. He thought I already knew this bit of information.

"I'll need to get the bluebook price and call you back. Is that okay?"

"That's fine. I'd like to get this settled by the end of the week. I'll wait to hear from you."

I had hung up the phone and immediately dialed her number

exclaiming, "Why didn't you tell me you were selling your car to Uncle Howard?"

"Cause you won't listen to me," she said. "I told you to sell it and you didn't."

After Howard bought the car, I stewed over her ways of getting me there to do things for her. Increasingly, I was called to take her to the grocery store, the ophthalmologist, the podiatrist, the internist, the radiologist, the hardware store, a church event. I was painting walls, putting down flooring, arranging for plumbers and electricians, changing heating and air conditioning filters and light bulbs, planting shrubs and flowers, mowing her lawn.

When new neighbors moved in next door, they often mowed her lawn. I felt my guilt mingle with my appreciation. I lived almost three hours away, was still working, and was there every week or ten days to do things for her. Her phone bill reflected multiple calls a day to me.

All this before her present impasse.

\* \* \*

"Beverly Ann. Beverly Ann," she calls – her voice coming to me as if out of a dream. "Where are you?"

I open the flamingo-colored front door, entering the living room of our cozy coastal cottage. She is standing with her arm on the back of "Larry's chair." I go to her, take her arm, saying, "Join Larry and me on the deck." We move slowly out the door, toward the third chair Larry has pulled up to join ours. "Tonight we'll watch the fireworks from these chairs," I say.

\* \* \*

On Monday morning, I am in the internist's office with her. Desiring an explanation for her hallucinations and recent emergency room visits, I ask, "Do you think my Aunt Sis' recent death has exacerbated my mother's anxiety?"

"Anything's possible," Dr. Robinson replies.

He is young – maybe my son's age. His words and tone convince me he cares about my mother. I do not begrudge the time we have spent in the waiting room because he is running behind schedule. Through the years, I have discovered that he lingers with his patients and has time for the questions of their caregivers. Dr. Robinson doesn't hurry. I am grateful to listen to a story he tells of his grandfather who is near the age of my mother. He is human, one of us. Over my mother's head in the examining room is a professional photograph of Dr. Robinson's baby daughter. I find it comforting.

I think to myself of all the losses my mother has experienced recently. Her two brothers, Curtis and Howard, her best friend of forty years, Violet, and her beloved sister-in-law, Sis, have all died in the last two and a half years, plus a number of cousins and acquaintances. Aunt Sis' May death was the most recent. My mother often said Aunt Sis was the sister she'd always prayed for. "When Sis was dating my brother, Curtis, she would always invite me to go along to the movies or to get a burger. Then they got married, and Sis was always there for me in good times and bad. I don't know what I would do without her."

I tell the doctor how I found her, why we are here, and how she has not improved significantly over the weekend.

He explains to me that she is in the early stages of dementia, based on some test results, her history of TIA's, and her recent behavior.

I ask the dreaded question. "Is it Alzheimers?"

"Not all dementia is Alzheimers. The only way to confirm it is with an autopsy. We won't call it that yet."

I like this doctor. He reminds me of a gentle bear. He smiles, asking a question while he warms his stethoscope with his hand before placing it on my mother's bare skin. He doesn't treat her as if she isn't there, even when she does not pay attention. He reports to me that she has lost weight in the past few months and asks her what she eats and how often.

When she doesn't answer, I find myself answering for her. "She used to eat a lot of fresh fruits and vegetables, chicken, fish, and red meat. Now she tends to buy a lot of T.V. dinners, diet drinks, cereal, peanut butter, and ice cream."

"Mrs. Brothers, is that true?" he asks.

"There's no one to cook for anymore," she answers.

Then it hits me. Of course. Uncle Curtis, Aunt Dot, and Uncle Howard used to drop in for a meal. She used to take food to Aunt Sis in the nursing home. They are gone now.

13

"Mrs. Brothers, given your weight loss, emergency room visits, and confusion, I think it's time for you to make a move to Pecan Groves Care Center. What do you think?"

To my surprise, she says, "I'm ready."

I don't know whether to sigh with relief or cry at this new forfeiture.

There in that clinic, I feel Artemis' arrow focused on my heart. Her steady aim and strong will ensure that she will reach her target. As the goddess of the hunt, Artemis is also the protectress. My heart is breaking wide open. My mother, who valued independence and taught me to be independent is becoming increasingly dependent. Artemis served as midwife to her mother, becoming the goddess of childbirth. Women called her "helper in pain." Can it be that the mother who gave birth to me now needs me to assist her in giving birth to this new cycle of her own life? Artemis, the goddess of wildlife and independence, represents the force of nature, the cycle of birth and death that continually repeats itself.

Later, I go to my copy of Anne Morrow Lindbergh's <u>Gift From the Sea</u> to find something I'd underlined just days ago – *"Perhaps this is the most important thing for me to take back from beach living: simply the memory that each cycle of the tide is valid, each cycle of the wave is valid, each cycle of a relationship is valid."*

My mother and I are in a metaphoric wilderness now and I am more aware of each of our vulnerabilities than I have ever been. Artemis, the Bear-Mother, had an outer fierceness that often covered her softer mothering qualities. My mother and I share a fierce determination, a sisterhood, and a strong sense of the self each wants to be. Our lives have been intertwined for so long. How do I hold on to me as I am letting go of her?

# CHAPTER TWO

## MOVING

## HESTIA

## GODDESS OF HOME HEARTH
## AND TEMPLE

*"To every woman who has kept a hearth....*
*I see Mothers, Grandmothers back to beginnings,*
*huddled beside holes in the earth....*
*Guarding the magic no other being has learned,*
*awed, reverent, before her sacred fire,*
*sharing live coals with the tribe."*
from Chains of Fire, Elsa Gidlow, the "poet warrior"

# Moving

"Mom, you are going to be moving today," I say.

"Today?" she questions.

We have left the doctor's office and are walking across the parking lot. The black asphalt radiates heat all around us as we head toward the car. I am grateful for this heat and think of the goddess, Hestia, keeper of the hearth.

For as long as I can remember, my mother has kept the home fires burning. The walls of any house she has ever occupied are like altars to the past and the future, decorated with family portraits. I recall Uncle Howard standing in her hall looking at a photo of himself, taken thirty years earlier, and one of his son, Glen, who was snatched from this earth at age twenty-two. "Sister," he'd said. "I know I can depend on you to always have my picture out."

When we reach the car I say, "Dr. Robinson said he'd call Pecan Groves Care Center to tell them we are on our way."

"I hate moving," she tells me. "Why would I want to move? I love my home."

"I know."

"I love my home. I hate moving." She repeats, as her eyes fill up with tears.

The voice in my head whispers, "Can she be at home in an institution?"

\* \* \*

Home was the source of many of my parents' angriest arguments. From the time I finished second grade until I started college, we lived in eleven different houses in six different towns. My dad, a plumber with a cowboy poet's heart, was a wanderer. There were many fights over dwelling places during my years living with them. My mother wanted to settle down in one town and own a home. Daddy had no such desire. The first fight I vividly remember was when I was seven.

"I want my own home," Mother screamed at Daddy, when he

announced we were selling the house they had built on a hill in Yoakum, and which we had occupied for two years. During the building process, they had argued over wallpaper patterns, flooring finishes, paint colors.... Finally, they had decided Momma would choose for the kitchen, master bedroom, and bathroom. Daddy would choose for the living room, dining room and exterior. Bobby and I would choose, with assistance, for our own rooms.

"I have a new job." Daddy said to her. "I'll be a traveling salesman for a plumbing supply house. It's best for you and the children to be close to your parents."

She was leaning against the sink, her dishwashing on pause. She had on a brown-and-white checked gingham housedress with a white collar trimmed in brown rickrack. She held a coffee cup, dripping soap bubbles and water. "Best for who?" she yelled. The crash of glass breaking interrupted the words. "I love this house. I helped clear the land to make a place for it. I don't want another home."

Though she was standing in her red-teapot, wallpapered kitchen, her sobs were so loud they traveled to the sand pile out back where I had escaped. When she screamed, Daddy just got quieter or went outside and saddled his horse to go riding. She frightened me when she screeched. I sat there longing for the Momma who could give me a day like one I had experienced earlier that week.

* * *

*"Rise and shine, "Momma exclaims as she pulls the covers back and tousles the hair on my head. "It's time to rise and shine. Breakfast's ready."*

*I can hear the radio playing WOAI. Momma loves to listen to the radio and to music on the record player. I follow her to the kitchen table where Daddy sits in his chair by the window reading the paper. I sit in my place. Bobby's chair on the other side is empty. Momma sings a second round of "rise and shine" for Bobby.*

*The table is covered with a red and yellow floral tablecloth and set with the everyday dishes, a pattern Momma is collecting from the grocery store. A pan of homemade biscuits, a platter of eggs over easy and bacon, real butter she made from the cream off the top of our own cow's milk, and a pitcher of syrup greet me. My cup, mostly milk with a little coffee, is sitting by my plate.*

Here comes Momma carrying Bobby. He just can't wake up. He is only three. I am five and Momma and Daddy have arranged for me to start first grade early.

Daddy puts down his paper and says, "Who wants to say the blessing?"

We don't eat until we say the blessing, usually one Bobby or I have just memorized at Sunday School. "Thank you for the world so sweet, thank you for the food we eat. Thank you for the birds that sing. Thank you God for everything. Amen." All four of us recite the blessing together.

Momma says, "You two are so smart. You memorize something the minute you hear it."

I love this breakfast. Sometimes we have oatmeal or cream of wheat and toast. On Sundays Momma makes pancakes or waffles or French toast and sausage. When we're sick, Daddy makes us milk toast. We finish our breakfast and Momma clears the table and stacks the dishes.

"I'll do these dishes after Bobby and I take Beverly Ann to school," she tells Daddy.

Somewhere between waking us up, making breakfast, and eating with us, Momma has made up all the beds and picked up our books and toys off the floor.

I go to my room and choose an outfit for the day at school. I would wear my little blue plaid suit everyday if I could. I love its pleated skirt and boxy jacket with the fancy buttons. Momma made it from a McCall's pattern. Since I wore it yesterday, I choose a navy blue dress with a gathered skirt, a sash that ties in a bow, smocking, and a white collar. Momma made it, too. She makes all my clothes except the ones I get as hand-me-downs from my older cousins, Barbara Jo and Nancy Kaye, whose momma, Azalea, shops for them at a store in San Antonio called Neiman's and at a fancy store called The Toggery.

"Beverly Ann, it's time to go," she calls.

I skip to the car and get in the front seat. Bobby is in the middle with our cat, Cocoa, on his lap. Bobby has on a hat and his underwear. That's what he wears most days. Momma lets him, except when it's cold.

Momma drops me off in front of the big steps at my elementary school. "I'll pick you up for lunch at 11:30, right here."

At 11:30 Momma's there with Bobby and we go home to lunch. Daddy is washing his hands at the sink. He is a plumber so his hands get very dirty. He washes them with Lava Soap which is very scratchy. He is wearing khakis that Momma starches and irons with a crease. Her laundry basket is full most of the time with all of our clothes that she's washed, starched, sprinkled, and is in the process of ironing.

Daddy says, "Baby, tell me something you learned in school this morning."

I have a long story today because my teacher, Mrs. Donnelly, took one of my classmates down to the bathroom and when she came back my classmate had on different clothes and her hair was damp. She smelled and looked better and she loved her new dress, a coral color like the one in my crayon box. It looked good with her blond hair.

Momma says to Daddy, "That must be that little Meyers girl. I bet she has lice. I don't know how that woman manages all those kids and her husband doesn't work a bit."

I love my teacher, Mrs. Donnelly. She is so nice. My momma and Mrs. Donnelly look alike. They both have black hair that is parted on the side and combed straight with just a little rolled up curl at the bottom. They both wear dresses that button up the front, have collars with a little v at the neck, and belts with buckles. Mrs. Donnelly wears high heels everyday but Momma only wears them on Sundays or when she is going to church or some place special.

For lunch we have smothered steak, creamed corn, green beans, jello salad, and homemade bread. We eat what Daddy likes. He buys the groceries.

In a vase on the table is a bouquet of sweet peas out of Momma's flower garden. It is a very big flower garden shaped like the letter L and it has sweet peas, bachelor buttons, gladiolas, baby carnations, marigolds, zinnias, roses, and hollyhocks. I get to pick flowers for my teacher some days. Momma loads up the trunk of the car with wash tubs sometimes and we go to get cow manure from my Uncle Curtis' dairy farm. When people ask what's her secret for getting such pretty flowers to grow in hard, black soil, Momma says, "It's the cow manure."

"Time to go back to school, honey," she says as she clears the table.

Daddy is still drinking his iced tea from his big goblet. She kisses him on the lips as she passes by. I love it when Momma and Daddy kiss and tease and hug.

Bobby wants to ride with us and that means Cocoa goes too. Sometimes Momma even lets Bobby take Sport, our border collie, in the car with us. Once when Sport's leg got run over by a car, Momma and Daddy worked *together to set it and nurse Sport back to almost good as new. They made Sport a splint and he limped around on it for a long time and then he didn't need it.*

*"Eddie, you should have been a veterinarian. You are so good with all of our animals," Momma often tells Daddy.*

*It's still recess when I get back from lunch. I run to play with my friends, Gaynelle. Connie, and Pauline. We have a "house" we made in the corner of the school yard with sticks, rocks, bits of broken glass, and Chinaberry leaves and berries. I just like to build the house. I don't like to play in it after it's built. Gaynelle, Connie, and Pauline are coming home with me after school today. Momma likes me to invite my friends over to play at our home, as she puts it.*

*Home, it seems, is the first thing in my momma's mind. Even though I'm aware that this home is important to her, I also know it is not about the house, not exactly.*

*Momma picks us up after school and when we get home we go into the kitchen to have a snack, milk and homemade oatmeal raisin cookies, my favorite. The milk is really cold the way I like it. I can smell supper cooking, pinto beans and cornbread.*

*My friends and I make up games. I know when Daddy gets home, we get to ride our horse, Lady, just once around the lot before Momma drives my friends home.*

*After supper, Bobby and I argue over who goes first for a bath, not wanting the day to be over. I lose and head for the tub while Daddy calls out,*

*"Remember to rinse the tub after you get out. No one wants to get into a dirty tub after someone else."*

*I pull on my yellow and pink flowered nightgown and find a stack of books ready to read. Momma bathes Bobby, and Daddy tells me to read him a story. Then Momma reads to Bobby and me from a chapter book we are reading each night, one about Lassie and a little boy, Timmy, being lost in a storm.*

*Bobby asks Momma, "Where is God when they're lost?"*
*She says, "God is with us even when we don't see Him."*
*Bobby says, "How do you know?"*
*Momma says, "I just have faith."*
*Bobby says, "What's faith?"*

*Momma says, "It's time for bed now."*

*Momma carries Bobby to his room to tuck him in. Daddy says the Lord's Prayer with me, and then Momma comes in and says, "Sweet dreams. See you in the morning." She turns off the light.*

\* \* \*

I can't escape from the mantra playing in my head. Can she be at home in an institution?

Before we can think of moving her, we must tend to the paperwork required by the nursing home. Dr. Robinson instructed us to leave his office and go directly to the admissions office at Pecan Groves Care Center.

As we enter the care facility, the smells of urine and pine-of-pine cleaner combine to greet us. I hear a woman's voice down a distant hall calling, "Help me. Help me." I have visited my aunt and uncle here in the past, so I know that the receptionist desk is to my left. Holding my mother by the hand, I walk to the desk and ask the scrubs-attired attendant, "Could you give me directions to the admissions office?"

"You just go down this hall," she says, pointing to her left. "It's the third door on the right. Does Sharon know you're coming?" she adds.

"Dr. Robinson said he'd call and tell her we were on our way," I reply.

I knock on the closed door.

"Come in," I hear.

Mother and I enter a small room with a single window. The admissions director sits behind a desk that faces the door. There are stacks of papers on the desk. On the bookshelf by the window are pictures of children.

Before I even introduce myself or my mother, I ask, "Are those your children?"

The admissions director smiles and says, "Yes. I have two girls and a boy."

"Me too," I tell her.

"I have lots of pictures of my children," my mother chimes in. She is holding her purse in her lap, sitting tall in her chair. *"Don't slump,"* I imagine her saying – a message from her throughout my youth.

"You'll have to put some of them up in your new home here," she replies.

She stands up, offers her hand to my mother, and introduces herself saying, "I'm Sharon."

"I'm Mrs. Brothers," my mother says. My mother never introduces herself by her first name to anyone younger.

"Have a seat here," Sharon offers, directing my mother to one of two chairs in front of the desk.

She extends her hand to me and says, "You must be Beverly. Dr. Robinson said you'd be bringing your mother over."

Seated in the admissions office with my mother beside me, I sign page after page from a stack on the desk. I feel responsible for her well-being and that motivates me to dwell on each document, read every word, and take in what I am doing.

"This is the last one," Sharon says as she hands me another piece of paper. "It's the DNR – Do Not Resusitate- form."

I had never dreamed of signing one of these. The gravity of doing so suddenly puts this move into perspective for me. *I am moving her to what might be her last home on this earth.*

I want to whisper in her ear, "Mother - fight, scream, yell. You have always battled for your own home, a place to stay put, as you would say. Why are you so silent now?"

The admissions director walks with us to Room 202 and leaves us at the door saying, "Mrs. Brothers, you have the bed by the window that looks out on the courtyard, as requested." This is important to both of us - - the bed by the window.

I go to the window and ask, "Mother, do you remember teaching me the names of trees and flowers? You always had the prettiest flower beds."

"I spent lots of hours in the yard digging, planting, weeding, and watering," she replies.

I am grateful to hear her response. She is with me right now.

"Come to the window," I say. "See the marigolds."

She joins me there and replies, "I never liked marigolds. I just planted them to keep the bugs out of my beds." She turns her back to the window and says, "I guess I'll never have a garden again."

A line from a Marge Piercy poem I'd recently written in my journal creeps into my mind – "*for every gardener knows that after the planting, after the long season of tending and growth, the harvest comes.*" She had to have the bed by the window.

"Let's go get some of your things for your new home here."

\* \* \*

Years of experience in moving has made it possible for us to make a comfortable space in a few hours. Today, we bought a new comforter and pillow sham for the bed. The quilted wedding ring design is ripe with flowers and vines in russets, golds, and greens.

"I like earth colors," she says, surveying stacks of comforters on the shelves.

We also purchased a new dormitory-sized refrigerator to hold her milk and soft drinks. It is sitting atop her nightstand for now, a reminder of the tight space she inhabits.

We are watching "The Sound of Music," thanks to having moved her television and VCR here earlier.

"Tomorrow, we'll go get some of your framed family photos to hang and your favorite blue chair," I promise.

She gets up, turning her back to me, saying, "There's not enough room in here."

"We'll need to bring more of your clothes, too."

"Are you spending the night here with me?" she asks.

"There's no bed for me."

"I don't want to be left alone."

"I'll sit here beside you until you fall asleep," I promise.

"No, you won't. You'll just leave me here all alone," she says, her voice suddenly more insistent.

"Mother," I tell her. "Calm down. I will help you get ready for bed."

"I don't want to get ready for bed," she yells! "Don't tell me what to do!"

"You don't have to put on your nightgown," I plead. "We'll just sit here and watch the rest of the movie together."

She sits on her bed, and before long she is stretched out and relaxed. I am in the chair beside her, holding her hand. She falls asleep with her clothes on.

"I'll be back first thing in the morning," I whisper as I let go of her hand and move toward the door.

The following morning I arrive with two poppy seed kolaches and two cups of coffee from the bakery. Mother is sitting at a mobile table with her untouched breakfast in front of her. She reaches for the bakery bag, grabs one of the kolaches, and bites into it, as if starving. She fumbles with the lid on one of the cups of coffee. I take it from her, remove the lid, and hand it back to her. I sit down on the bed and hear the crunch of the plastic covered mattress. Her tray is between us. I remove the lid from my cup of coffee and take a sip of this tasteless brew. She reaches for the second roll. I had intended that one for myself, imagining us having conversation, coffee, and a roll together as we planned our second moving day. I watch as she devours it.

"Why didn't you have breakfast in the dining room?" I inquire.

"I didn't want to."

Taking a deep breath, I say, "Where is your roommate?"

"I don't know."

She is wearing the same clothes she had on yesterday. This is not my mother. My mother loves to choose something new to wear each day. *"Never wear the same thing two days in a row," I hear her thirty-something self say to my little girl.* I decide not to question her attire.

"Let's go pick up some more things from your house and bring them over here."

"I want my blue chair."

I am grateful for a cousin with a truck who is moving that for her today.

"I want some of my mugs. I don't like drinking coffee from styrofoam," she declares, putting down the cup I'd brought in from the bakery.

"I agree with you, Mom. I don't like drinking from styrofoam cups either."

\* \* \*

Where is the "old Beverly", the one who would say something sarcastic to her, like "You are certainly demanding, aren't you?" She must be in hibernation right now. Thank goodness. I feel such compassion for my mother right now. This has to be incredibly hard for her. It's killing me, and I'm just the one bearing witness.

I say a word of thanks to Hestia, goddess of home and hearth, who transforms the mundane into the sacred. When I had called up the mundane details of an ideal day from the childhood home created by my mother, was I yearning for both my mother and me to have that feeling of being at home with ourselves, regardless of where we actually resided? Hestia offers us a center, a place to be protected from the outside world, a home that no one or no thing can invade. My mother will need such a center if she is to reside here in this institutional space, occupied by the aging, waiting. Waiting for what? I will need such a center if I am to bear witness to this move, if I am to accompany her on this journey.

* * *

My mother finally made her dream come true. In 1965, she talked Daddy into making the down payment on the house they lived in until my father passed over in 1976. She prided herself in keeping him *at home* during a lengthy bedridden existence. It was this house in which she lived the longest - until 1998 – thirty-three years in one house in one town, a town she loved, San Marcos. The San Marcos house was her true home in many aspects. It was the place where she discovered she could do work she loved, make her own money, pay her own house payments, eat food she chose, watch her favorite movies and TV shows, take weekend trips with women friends, choose paint and curtains and furniture without consulting another, and sit on her bed underlining in red her favorite Bible passages. Like Hestia, she was owning herself. Beware to anyone who threatened her home, her autonomy, her dwelling place.

* * *

Back at her house, we work together. She chooses a few, from the many photographs of her two brothers, our original family of four, grandchildren, and great-grandchildren. Then she asks, "Did you pack the pictures of the brides and the babies?"

I assure her they are in the box. Her request is no surprise to me. She is a celebrator of events. Births, baptisms, the first day of school, graduations, weddings, New Year's, Valentine's, St. Patrick's, Easter,

Fourth of July, Halloween, Thanksgiving, Christmas are all celebrated in her home. Decorating for holidays is part of her legacy to me.

* * *

*While packing, I ask my mother,. "Do you remember when I was in fourth grade you hosted a Valentines Day tea party for me and my friends. You decorated homemade tea cakes with pink and red buttercream frosting and let me put sparkly red and silver sprinkles on top. You served fruit punch in little crystal cups and created party favors from doilies, construction paper, and red heart-shaped lollipops. Dressed in your Sunday clothes, a red wool crepe dress you'd sewn for yourself and your black suede pumps, you served us. We all wore red or pink as the party invitation requested. It was 1953 and girls in South Central Texas wore dresses to school unless it was freezing cold. You didn't blink an eye when we giggled and raced from the lace covered dining table you'd so carefully prepared to the horse pen to feed Billy and Cookie some of the refreshments you'd made.*

* * *

"Do you remember that?"

She laughs and says, "We better get busy. There's more to do."

The day goes by quickly and I am feeling some relief. Maybe she is adjusting. We have taken some of her things to the nursing home, but we have left most of her things in her home.

I find consolation in telling her, "Let's leave the house like you have it now. We'll come back often and spend the night."

I am not surprised to hear her approval.

"That's a great idea," she affirms.

Why wasn't I prepared for the tantrum when we returned to the nursing home?

I pull into the parking lot, get out of the car, walk around to open her door and assist her, only to be greeted with, "Take me home."

"This is where you live now," I assert.

"I don't live here," she screams, jerking her arm from my hand.

I look up to see a couple of staff smoking cigarettes in the designated smoking area. I imagine them saying, "How cruel. Show your mother some respect."

"Yes, you live here now," I say as I take her arm.

"I hate you. You are not my daughter. If you loved me, you would take me home."

I close her door, walk around to the driver's side, and get into the car. It is hot so I turn on the air conditioner. I think she'll calm down and go in with me if I just sit and wait awhile. When her sobbing and accusations continue, I decide to drive around town.

I distract her by pointing out familiar places, like the courthouse or the park, hoping she will tire of her own resistance.

Finally, I pull up to the nursing home again, and say, "Mother, it will be dark soon and I have a long drive ahead of me. Larry is expecting me home tonight."

Home. Where is home? The cliché, "Home is where the heart is," echoes in my head. John Denver's long ago hit comes to mind – "Country roads, take me home…" as "Home again, home again, piggedy pig…" competes for my attention.

She says, "I don't want you driving in the dark. Call Larry and tell him you'll come home tomorrow."

"No," I say.

I get out of the car, cross over to the passenger door, open it, unhook her seat belt, and take her hand. Amazingly, she lets me help her up from the car seat and out the car door. We walk into the nursing home where the dinner smells mingle with human smells. I take her to her assigned seat in the dining room, kiss her, saying, "Today is Tuesday. I'll be back on Friday. I love you."

I am afraid my courage will vanish if I don't leave right now. I leave without looking back.

\* \* \*

I begin my drive home. An hour out of town, I pull over to the side of the road. I am sobbing so hard that my nose is running and my chest heaves. I concentrate on my breathing. I am consumed by grief.

As is my habit, I called my husband, Larry, when I left Hallettsville so he would know when to expect me. Now, I'm not even sure how long I have been sitting here on the side of the road. It is dark. I want to talk to my brother, Bobby. I want to hear his words come out slowly, carefully, reassuring me that everything is as I remember it. Mother always hated moving and she had to move so many times. It filled her with rage. Bobby and I beheld that rage many times. We shared a reality. On occasion in our adult lives, we have verified those experiences with one another. I have just moved our mother again. Will the rage return? Or has it been vanquished by the Ativan she takes to keep the demon/daemon at bay. What is that demon/daemon? Could it be, I wonder, that she feels squeezed out of her life? Does she feel, literally and metaphorically, without a home, a place to call her own?

No doubt, she determined that *I* would have a place of my own, literally and metaphorically, when she said to me upon the occasion of my showing her my freshman schedule, "You *won't* take homemaking. That's a waste of time. Any fool can cook and sew. You need to prepare for college and a career."

She drove me back to the high school where, at her instruction, I went in and substituted Latin I for the homemaking class I had thought I'd take with my friends.

When I look back, thinking of that day I wonder how she could think of herself as a fool. At the time, she was a full-time homemaker, filling her days with cooking, sewing, cleaning, laundering. She said one thing, but I saw her doing another. Which message was the true message? Could I do both, have a career and a home? I was confused.

It is no wonder I was confused. Like Hestia, my mother treated home as a temple, cleaning and decorating as if honoring the Divine. However, the messes made by those of us who also lived in the home space she created often made her efforts feel futile and disrespected. She would lose her temper and admonish us for our unappreciative behaviors. The fire on the hearth would be extinguished in these moments, and I would retreat to my own center, waiting until it was safe to return. I was learning how to build my own home. Decades later, I would read these words from John O'Donohue's *Blessing for a New Home* – "*May this home be a place of discovery, /Where the possibilities that sleep/ In the clay of your soul can emerge/ To deepen and refine your vision/ For all that is yet to come to birth.*"

Like the ancients, I had set out from my childhood home with fire from the common hearth to ignite the hearth in my own home, linking the past with the present. I spent years in therapy trying to analyze and understand the home I grew up in and its effect on the home I was creating for myself and *my* family. I would need Hestia's presence to remind me of the gifts that home brought to my soul. Now I realized I was calling on the goddess of hearth and home to be with me and my mother during this current move to the nursing home. Daddy wasn't moving her this time. I was. What did I need from Hestia? What did my mother need from Hestia? Is the answer as simple as – *to know thyself?*

And I remember this: Hestia does not flaunt a persona. Hestia is an essence, not a form. I love the dictionary definition of essence – *that which makes a thing what it is.* Getting to the essence of something takes time and discernment. I have spent a lifetime attempting to get to the essence of my mother and myself. Home was one aspect of my mother's essence – Hestia incarnate in her love of home, but home always wrested from others, like my father?

# CHAPTER THREE

## ONCE UPON A TIME

## APHRODITE

## GODDESS OF SENSUALITY, LOVE, BEAUTY, AND SEXUALITY

*"….I feel, that is all.*
*I love.*
*The force of my love would carry me*
*to the ends of the earth."*
from Revelations: Diaries of Women,
ed. Maryjane Moffat and Charlotte Painter

# Once Upon A Time

My mother has been in the nursing home six months. I am visiting her today, on what would have been my parents' sixty-first wedding anniversary. In the living room at the nursing home, my mother speaks to Henry, a nursing home acquaintance, who is headed to his girlfriend's room. Henry and his girlfriend, June, frequently sit in this room, on the sofa, snuggled up, quietly together, occasionally kissing. I am touched by the tenderness of Henry when June clearly has Alzheimers.

"Hi, Henry," my mother calls out.

"Good afternoon, Charlyne," he replies.

After he has disappeared, she says, "He's having an affair with that woman. You know which one I mean."

"They're both single. It's not an affair," I assert.

"Call it what you want. They're not married. Having sex when you're not married is an affair to me."

I take a deep breath, stifling a sigh.

"The first time your daddy strayed," my mother says, glancing up at me, "at least the first one I know of, I found out from Aunt Doll. I was her namesake and she couldn't keep a secret like that from me."

"I don't need to know that. I had my own relationship with Daddy. That was between you and him."

Anger catches and burns in my throat. Daddy has been dead for years. Why is she telling me this *again, now*? On their anniversary, no less.

"Don't act like a spoiled baby. You're a grown woman. These things happen."

I am astounded that she is talking to me like this. I am a woman whose first husband left with another woman. I know about these things. I just don't want to discuss them with my mother, especially in the public living room of the nursing home. Her words just reinforce what I already think and feel – she doesn't know me or see me or hear me. In her eyes, I am her invention.

"He was with his girlfriend when you broke your arm," she says.

"Stop!" I tell her. "I don't want to hear this."

I look around to see people in wheelchairs staring at us instead of the television screen that usually captures their attention. Conversations about sex are always attention getting.

\* \* \*

Maybe it's because my mother is a Scorpio. Talking about sex has never been a taboo with her. She had wanted to make sure I understood, in advance, what my menstrual period would look like, and that I would be prepared for it *before* they showed the film to my fifth grade class at school. That was followed by the eighth grade talk about sexual intercourse and babies. I wanted her to shut up. I wasn't going to have a baby anytime soon. She and Daddy had already said I couldn't even date until I was sixteen. Later, when I was dating, she said, "Sex is beautiful and a wonderful expression between two people who love one another and are committed to creating a married life together."

There was also the warning, "You have to be the one to say *no*. You choose when and who you say *yes* to. There are consequences to your behaviors."

That statement has the stamp of Aphrodite on it. Aphrodite is mistress of her own love life. Contrary to popular belief, Aphrodite is not a reckless, romance driven goddess. She is protective of her children, lovers, and husband. She offers her divine touch of love, something we humans desire, the divine spark that lets our hearts speak freely and offer love without bondage.

My parents definitely sparked each other. They were at home in their bodies. They liked to dress up, keep fit, look good. As long as I can remember, my mother has repeated, unsolicited, "Your daddy was the handsomest man in the county."

I recall a time a few years ago when my husband, Larry, had put on a little weight that settled in his stomach. My mother was visiting and advised him, saying, "Larry, you'd never have seen Eddie Brothers with a belly hanging over his belt. You could lose a little weight."

"You sure know how to hurt a guy," Larry zipped back at her.

Undeterred, she'd said, "Fat doesn't look good and it isn't healthy either."

Later, I'd apologized to Larry for what my mother said.

"Larry, I'm so sorry you had to listen to that. My adolescence was full of *don't gain weight* lectures. I hated them."

Those weren't the only lectures I received. My parents were of a generation who believed in appropriateness, and belonged to a church that believed in hell and preached no dancing, drinking, fornication.... I have a list of "My Momma Says..." in my head for easy reference. "There are some girls men hang out with and some girls men marry. They are two different kinds of girls." That was usually followed by, "Being a lady is a desirable goal. Ladies have manners. They don't smoke, curse, drink alcohol, or bleach their hair." Those were all signs of "trashy' behavior.

I once challenged her, arguing, "You love Aunt Benelle and she smokes, drinks, and dyes her hair."

"Don't talk back," she commanded.

* * *

How did love and sex and drinking and smoking and dancing and dyed hair all get mixed up together? Could it be that Aphrodite's delight in the gratification of the senses is present here? Her attraction to experience is a facet in women who appreciate the sensory gifts of life.

Aphrodite is alive and well in this nursing home. Women roam the halls rouged and lipsticked. One day, an eighty-something man comes up beside me, takes my hand, and says, "I'm Ray. What's your name?" He reeks of Aqua Velva.

I say, "Beverly," and try to wrest my hand from his grip. "Ray, I'm on the way to see my mother. It was nice to meet you."

Still holding on, he says, "You have pretty eyes."

"Thanks, Ray. I'll see you later." I take my free hand and remove my other from his hold.

* * *

Aware that the living room is filling up with folks who are coming in to wait until dinner, I suggest to Mother, "Let's go for a ride and have dinner out." She has on her favorite red-and-white paisley, long-sleeved blouse with a scarf-like collar over a pair of black slacks. She has worn long sleeves, summer and winter, fall and spring, since her mastectomy in 1984. She has on makeup and pearl earbobs.

35

"I'll need my coat. It's cold out."

"I'll get it from your room. Wait here," I say.

Everything takes her longer these days, and I am ready to be out of this room in this nursing home listening to my mother tell me about my daddy's infidelities.

I return with her coat, help her put it on, and we move toward the door, down the sidewalk, to my car.

I open the door, help her in, and say, "While we are riding, you can tell me about the blizzard on your wedding day." It is a story I know by heart but I want to hear her tell it to me again, today.

"You know the story," she utters.

It is late afternoon, not her best time. I am not going to hear the story from her. I tell her story to her, remembering it from the many times I've heard it before.

\* \* \*

*You and Daddy went to the Baptist parsonage in Shiner to be married. The only people there with you were Daddy's cousin, Robert Lee, and his wife, Azalea. They were your witnesses. It was wartime and winter and you had chosen a navy blue wool suit with decorative stitching and a small navy blue hat which barely showed in your black hair. You wore black kid high-heeled pumps and silk hosiery which was hard to get. Daddy gave you a pink rose corsage, though yellow roses were your favorite. Daddy had on his custom-made boots, a suit he'd purchased at Joske's in San Antonio, a white starched shirt, and a striped tie. He'd removed his Stetson hat when he entered the parsonage. After the wedding, you walked out into the beginning of a Texas style blizzard, freezing cold wind and sleet burned your face. You all ran to Robert Lee's two door-car and you and Daddy climbed into the back seat. You drove to Slayden and spent the night in Daddy's boyhood home. He sang, "Baby, it's cold outside..." to you when he woke you up the next morning to a ten-degree temperature outside.*

\* \* \*

"Did I get it right?" I ask.

"Sounded fine to me. Could you turn up the heat? I'm cold."

"I'll do that."

36

"Where are we going to eat?"

"What are you in the mood for?

"I want a seafood platter."

"We'll have to drive out-of-town for that."

"We have plenty of time," she replies.

I drive twenty miles to a restaurant that serves a seafood platter. Inside, we are seated and she orders. When her plate arrives, on it are stacked fried oysters, shrimp, fish, coleslaw, and potatoes. She cleans her plate. On our drive back, she asks me to stop at a local convenience store to get her some Pepto Bismol. I stop, and when I return to the car with the pink stomach soother, she is vomiting onto the black asphalt, her head hanging away from the open door.

"I sure enjoyed it the first time," she laughs. "Not so much the second."

I can't decide whether to laugh or cry. I hand her the bottle. She pours it into the little plastic cup that comes attached to the lid. She swallows. Her hand is shaking. She pulls out a packaged wet one from her purse and wipes her face. Her purse has always contained wet ones, toothpicks, bandaids, Dentyne Lifesavers, Kleenex, cash, a travel sewing kit, pens, notepad, Benadryl, Campho Phenique, and Tylenol because she's allergic to aspirin.

Few of those things are in her purse now. The nursing home required removal of toothpicks, the travel sewing kit, Tylenol, Benadryl, and Campho Phenique.

I can't imagine her without all the things to care for the physical needs of herself and those she loves. Aphrodite women don't care if they have known you for a minute or an hour or a lifetime, they are fully, humanly present to you and the moment. All of their senses are engaged. They are there for you.

I am reminded of how I have often been embarrassed by this part of my mother, the part that is so consumed by human bodily needs.

\* \* \*

As soon as I became engaged she announced, "I made you an appointment with Dr. Booker for a physical examination and birth control pills."

"I can make my own appointment," I replied. *Now she's making my contraceptive plan for me,* I thought.

"It's already done - next Monday at 3:00."

"I'm going alone," I declare.

"Suit yourself. I already told him you were engaged, getting married in November, and needed birth control pills."

"I could have told him myself."

"Getting pregnant before you're married can ruin your life. Mark my word, that's not going to happen to you."

How could it, given my parents and the Southern Baptist Church? We Baptist girls talked about how we'd done everything but "IT," as intercourse was so euphemistically referred to.

"Girls who aren't virgins before marriage are a disgrace to the white dresses they wear down the aisle," she continued.

"Why didn't you wear a white dress when you were married?" I wanted to scream at her. Instead, I went to my room, and imagined why she hadn't.

What was my mother attracted to when she met my father? Was it his green eyes that gleamed from his olive-skinned face, framed by his soft black hair? Was it his easy way with words? His ability to make you feel heard while he was sitting and listening to you? His generosity with his time, money, and energy? His family's comfort in the world? His dreams?

What did Daddy see in my mother that caused him to end thirty-six years of bachelorhood? Was it her saucer-sized deep blue eyes in her oval fair-skinned face surrounded by jet black hair? Was it her ability to start a conversation with a total stranger? Her skill at creating beauty? Her ease with and love of children? Her story-telling mastery? Her sense of humor and practical joking? Her ambition?

Or was it lust? Passion? Were they kissed by Aphrodite, the goddess of unrestrained sexuality, beauty, and femininity? The touch of Aphrodite is not rational. A mutual attraction, the thing we call chemistry, can cause a transformation of the two people. I remember being on the periphery of their passion, seeing the pull toward one another as it manifested in a kiss, a shoulder rub, a hug, a jealous argument over a perceived flirtation with another.

Lots of questions float around, unasked, in my head. Why were

Daddy's cousins the only ones present for their wedding ceremony? Where were their parents? Their siblings? Why did they get married at a parsonage in a town in the geographic middle of their two hometowns instead of marrying in a church in her hometown? If she was a Methodist, why did a Baptist minister marry them?

When I get to that last question, I do know the answer. Daddy was almost fifteen years older than Momma when they married. He was a Baptist. He wanted to be married by a Baptist minister. She was in love. She did what he asked. For a while anyway.

* * *

I return her to the nursing home after dinner, never having asked her any of the questions I'd been pondering today, on their anniversary. At her house, I spend the night alone. I take my journal to the sofa in the living room, where I curl up to write down stories she has told, and my imaginations of what their falling in love was all about.

My mother believed in fairy tales. She thought her prince would come and her life would be transformed. When the goddess, Aphrodite, is present, the woman is in love with being in love. An Aphrodite woman may leave behind more than one lover, something most women of my mother's generation did not often talk about with others. I, certainly, believed my daddy was my mother's *first* love. Hearing her tell their stories was like listening to a beloved fairy tale. I borrow her words and write my own "Once Upon A Time" to assist me in understanding who they were and what attracted them to one another.

* * *

*It is 1942.*

*"Charlyne, I want you to meet my brother, Eddie," Benelle exclaims one spring day. The two of them are visiting on the porch of Charlyne's parents' house where she lives.. "He'll be in town on the weekend. You could come over for dinner."*

*"Sounds nice," Charlyne replies. "Could I bring something?"*

*"Bring some of those delicious homemade rolls you're known for making."*

*"Anything else?"*

"Dessert. A pie or something."

The week is filled with plans for the date. Charlyne sews herself a new pale blue chambray sundress, knowing the blue will make her eyes pop. She has a pair of white strappy sandals that will look good with the dress. "I'll wear my pearl earbobs and necklace," she says to herself in the mirror. She puts a record on the Victrola and listens to Frank Sinatra croon. She is twenty-one and feels like a teenager again.

The date night arrives and Charlyne prepares. She bathes with Ivory, dusts herself with Forever Yours talcum powder, puts on her prettiest lingerie, buttons up the front of her new dress, slips on her sandals, fastens her pearls, positions her earbobs, colors her lips with Tangee, and twirls in front of the mirror. She tells her parents good night, closes the screen door behind her, and walks the few blocks to Benelle and Hilmer's to meet Eddie. She has her rolls and cherry pie in a basket lined with a dish towel she has embroidered. Benelle and Patty, her four year old, greet Charlyne at the door. Benelle gushes over the pretty embroidered dish towel and her talent for sewing and baking. Patty pulls her into the living room.

Eddie stands up, walks over to her, takes her hand and says, "You must be Charlyne. My sister is a fan of yours. I'm Eddie. No telling what you've heard about me."

She is smitten. He is so handsome. No one has ever said she was worthy of a fan. He is so self-assured. And, the touch of his hand. Please, God, let this be the one, she thinks. Plus, she loves his sister too.

Benelle has set the table with her best dishes -- her mother's wedding china -- pure white with a gold rim. "I'm the one she knew would use them," Benelle says, explaining why the youngest of four received the family china. There are flowers in the center of the table, daisies mixed with yellow roses. The smell of roasting meat fills the room. "You know I don't have time to cook these days, so Nora came to help with the meal. My dance and expression school takes too much time. Thanks for bringing the rolls and pie."

Eddie holds the chair out for her. She sits. Patty clamors to sit beside Charlyne. Eddie says, "I'm not arguing with the princess. I'll sit across from our guest. I'll have a better view of those blue eyes."

The evening draws to a close and Eddie says, "Why don't I walk you home?"

"Thanks. That would be nice."

By the end of the year they are engaged. It has been a year of weekends *together and weekdays apart. The weekends are romantic, filled with dances and friends and talk. She's never known a man with dreams as big as hers, and the daring to say them out loud. Though her mother warns her about the age difference - "He's thirty-six and you are only twenty-one." - she listens to her heart. She has known a lot of heartbreak for a twenty-one year old, and she refuses to let that keep her from enjoying the fluttering of her heart now. She's in love.*

It is now midnight, I put away my journal, turn off the light, and sleep.

\* \* \*

The following morning, I stop at the nursing home on my way back to Port Aransas.

At the door to her room, I pause and listen to her argue with a nurse's aide.

"I'm not taking a shower here. My daughter will take me home to bathe."

"Mrs. Brothers, you have to have a shower today. It's your day on the schedule."

"I can shower myself. I don't need your help."

"We can't leave you alone in the shower. That's the law."

Bursting into tears, she cries, "I don't want you to touch me. Leave me alone."

"Is there a problem here?" I ask as I move toward the two of them. The aide is young, maybe even in her late teens. She has on pink scrubs with butterflies and flowers sprinkled on the fabric. She is several inches taller than my mother and speaks in an authoritative voice for someone so young. I think to myself that she will need that voice and demeanor to get my mother to do something she clearly doesn't want to do.

"It's your mother's shower day and she isn't cooperating."

Mother is dressed for her day. It is eight in the morning and she has probably been up for several hours.

"I don't want to take a public shower." She looks directly at the aide, hands on her hips, and warns, "I don't want you touching me. I don't even know you."

Aphrodite is in the room with us now. Relatedness is essential to understanding the Aphrodite woman. If you are not relating to her, she is not interested in what you have to say or do. Rules and schedules don't appeal to an Aphrodite woman. The patriarchy has, historically, made rules. The Aphrodite in my mother has, historically, disobeyed them.

"Mom, calm down," I say.

"Don't tell me to calm down. I want to take a bath with my Zest soap and strawberry shampoo. I don't want to take a shower here. I don't like showers. I like baths."

To the aide, I say, "It's okay. You can go. I'm here now."

She says, "If she doesn't take a shower today, she doesn't get one until the end of the week. That's the schedule."

I already know I will forego my plans to just stop in, say hi, and drive home this morning. I am going to take my mother home for a bath. Then we will stop at Wal-Mart and buy her Zest soap and strawberry shampoo to bring back here for the next assigned shower day.

* * *

I remember as a child going into the bathroom after Momma had taken her bath. The room was steamy, the mirrors fogged, the fruit and flower fragrances exaggerated by the heat.

When my parents built the house on the hill, Momma said, "I want a blue and yellow bathroom with a black and white tile floor. She kept it sparkling clean. She would emerge from that room in her flowered robe, tied at the waist, and sit at her dressing table to put on her makeup and fix her hair. I would linger on the periphery, watching her.

One night she was dressing for her Sunday School Class Christmas party and she tied a celadon scarf at her neck and sat gazing into the mirror. I said, "You look beautiful."

She said, "I feel pretty tonight."

I felt happy. Just the month before, Daddy had given Momma a black silk crepe robe with pale blue satin piping trim around the collar, the cuffs, and on the pockets. It was her birthday present. I thought it was *so glamorous*, like something Ava Gardner or Cyd Charisse would wear in the movies.

When she opened the package with the robe in it, she started crying. Then she threw the package down and left the room.

Daddy followed her and I could hear them arguing.

"I never do anything right, do I?" Daddy asked.

"You know I'll never wear a robe like that. It's not me. It's for some picture of me you have in your head. I'll never be that woman. Is that the woman you want?" Her voice got louder. That was Bobby's and my cue to leave the house for the out-of-doors.

"Momma's mad again," I said to Bobby as we headed to the horse pen.

"I know." He kicked at a rock.

"It makes me sad. I like it when Momma and Daddy are nice to each other."

"Me, too." He picked up a rock and threw it against the cow shed.

What went on between the two of them in the privacy of their bedroom was not even something two little kids would ever speculate on. What we did know was that they went there to "talk." Today's talk was not a pleasant one. *Did* Daddy want a different woman than Momma?

There were no *Playboy-like* magazines on my daddy's nightstand, though I found a book on sexual relationships in my parents' chest of drawers during one of my snoopy periods around age thirteen.

My friend, Sammie, had encouraged me to look. "I just found a book about sex in my parents' bedroom," she confided. "I bet if you look, you'll find one too."

Later, at a slumber party at her house, six of us talked about what we had learned from the books. Other girls, besides Sammie and me, had snooped also. Aphrodite had anointed us with desire. Our curiosity stimulated a need to know. What did men and women do when they were in love and alone with each other?

\* \* \*

Mother and I return from our trip to her house to take a bath. As we enter the hall on which her room is located, an elderly, bald man, who comes to my shoulder, hurries toward us smiling.

"Look at that old coot. He can't wait to get down here to see you."

"Shh, he'll hear you," I reply. " I like Mr. James."

"He likes you, too. You'd think he'd be too old for that. He must be ninety."

"He *is* ninety. He told me that the last time I visited." Is my mother jealous?

Mr. James and I met when he was my uncle's roommate here. I

enjoy visiting with him. He collects inspirational stories and quotations, something we have in common, so we exchange them on occasion. He has pieces of art on the shelves in his room. Curious about a lovely walnut box inlaid with silver and turquoise, I'd recently asked if there was a story that went with it.

"Sure is," he'd replied. "That box contains my wife's ashes. We both loved to fish on the Pecos River in New Mexico so we made a pact to have our ashes spread there at the same time. I'm keeping them until mine can be mingled with hers and our son can sprinkle them in the Pecos. I miss her every day."

A love story. I so enjoy a good love story. What I longed for as a child was parents who were creating a love story together. My parents were full of the passion of Aphrodite, but I longed for them to show me the other aspects of that goddess - the loving presence that would melt down all walls and barriers and render them vulnerable and defenseless, soft and open. I wanted to see them show each other their tender parts, and then shine that warmth on my brother and me.

"Hi, Mr. James," I say and give him a hug.

"Did you two ladies go out for lunch?"

"We sure did. We had a morning of errands followed by lunch out."

At my side, Mother is punching me as if she thinks he can't see her impatience and rudeness.

"Mrs. Brothers," he says, "You look pretty today. That red dress becomes you."

I almost expect my mother to say *hrrump, what do you know,* but she replies, "Thank you," and even smiles.

After all, this is the same mother who bought me *Seventeen* and *Vogue,* picking out dresses she liked, to sew for me, without a pattern. She likes a compliment on her appearance. She likes a dress that gets noticed. Like Aphrodite, she appreciates beauty and a compliment from an appreciative admirer.

My prom dress was a creation of hers from a picture in *Vogue.* "You'll have the only one like this," she'd proudly announced as she showed me the picture and fabric. I had to admit I loved that dress with its black taffeta floor length skirt, white lace bodice, and wide pink satin cumberbund.

Her gifts, handmade, showed Aphrodite's influence. At Christmas she sewed taffeta monogrammed house shoes -- "scuffs" -- or lavender filled sachets for female relatives and teachers. She whipped paraffin, laced it with glitter, and made holiday candles for decoration. One Christmas I awoke to a new bride doll surrounded by my other dolls, all dressed in pastel net and satin bridesmaid's dresses she'd made to complete the wedding party.

She also read tips in magazines and clipped out hints to give me, ensuring I would remember - places to dab your perfume, posture when seated on a stage, glossy hair care, makeup suggestions for certain face shapes.... The night before my second wedding she gave me a gift of sheer lingerie. All hints of Aphrodite's presence in her life.

Mother has always liked to look good. As I approached my teens, her looks combined with her "never meets a stranger" personality often prompted Daddy to accuse her of being flirtatious. They would return from a party or even a family gathering, and I would hear him say, "You know you were flirting with him. Don't deny it." She was thirty-seven when I turned thirteen and Daddy was almost fifty-two. Age was beginning to be an issue.

I would move out of earshot, regardless of the time of night or day. I left the house and headed to the yard or to sit in the car or maybe I put a pillow over my ears. I knew there was a war going on in our house and I wanted to stay out of it.

\* \* \*

Just a few years ago, Larry and I had invited Lou, a recently widowed, seventy something friend of ours, to have Thanksgiving with us. It was just the four of us, Mother, Lou, Larry, and me. We had fresh flowers and candles on the table, music playing softly in the background, and when Lou pulled Mother's chair out for her, she actually blushed.

More friends joined us for dessert later and stories, jokes, and laughter filled the air. After everyone had departed and we were cleaning up, Mother said, "That Lou is a rounder, I can tell."

"Really," I replied. I was intrigued by her response to this man. "What makes you say that?"

"I can just tell. How do y'all know him?"

"Larry and Lou take watercolor lessons together at a gallery in

Rockport every week. They have a commute and they've become buddies."

"He was devoted to his wife who recently died of cancer," I said. "They were so attentive to one another." I'm thinking to myself of the passion so evident between Lou and Liz. They held hands, they bickered, they took their chairs and drinks to the beach in the late afternoon and sat side by side watching the waves come and go, and they ran a business together. When she died, Lou was so alone and lonely. They had each left another relationship to be together and had created a new life for just the two of them. He told us of being there, holding her to him when she passed.

My mother's voice interrupts my thoughts. "I don't think you can tell from the outside looking in about other people's relationships. There's always more than meets the eye."

"You're probably right," I agree, not wanting an argument at the end of this wonderful evening.

Aphrodite is never far from the antics of the god of war, Mars. Maybe that is because women were often among the spoils of war. Think of all the stories that combine love and war - Antony and Cleopatra, Lancelot and Guinevere, Napoleon and Josephine, Rhett

and Scarlett. Is my mother still at war with her attraction to men and her desire to be a free and powerful and independent woman?

\* \* \*

Wondering takes me back to age eight and our neighbors, the Jensons. Mrs. Jenson had two kids a little younger than my brother and me. Her husband worked at a feed store in town. One evening, I heard Momma say to Daddy, "Something's wrong with that woman. She goes around all day looking like something the cat drug in, but the minute he walks in the door at 5:15, she's all fixed up like she's going out for the evening. Why doesn't she think enough of herself to look nice all day?"

Daddy just drank his iced tea and didn't say anything.

"Well, Eddie Brothers, I want you to know, I dress for myself, not just for you."

"I can appreciate that, Charlyne," he replied.

I was only eight but I could feel a storm brewing.

* * *

I'm glad I took the time to take her home for a bath this morning. I won't do it every day but I did it today. Truthfully, I know it's possible that there will be more shower wars. Mother does not give in easily.

Living with Aphrodite is difficult and sometimes painful for a modern woman. In our family, Aphrodite's wound goes back for generations, clashing with the rule making patriarchy alive and well in both my maternal and paternal families, and in the institutions like this nursing home where she resides. In this journey toward the end, Mother and I will both need to continue to dress up, go out, see, hear, smell, taste, and touch all that this human life on earth offers. We will need to savor the senses we have. Aphrodite would approve of that.

# CHAPTER FOUR

## MAKE A LIFE OF YOUR OWN

## ATHENA

## GODDESS OF WISDOM, CRAFTS, DISCERNMENT, AND LEADERSHIP

*"I don't wish women to have power over men –
but over themselves."*
– Simone De Beauvoir, French existentialist
philosopher and writer

Year Two

# Make A Life of Your Own

It is Good Friday. The trees are budding, except for the mesquite. As I drive to visit my mother, I am reminded of another of her horticulture lessons. "Winter's not really over until the mesquite trees start budding." Here, in the fields beside this road, they obviously are not budding. This has been a long winter with many trips back and forth to manage my mother's increasing needs, and now the mesquites aren't green yet. I am taking my mother home with me for the Easter weekend.

I arrive this morning to find her phone missing from her room. At the nurses' station I ask where it might be. "We had to unplug it and remove it from her room. She called 911 for the third time last night," Jeannine, who I've gotten to know this winter, tells me.

"What?" I ask in alarm. "*Third* time? You mean she's done this before? Why didn't anyone tell me?

"We didn't want to bother you, and we thought it would stop. It hasn't, so we need to ask you to cancel her phone service. We can't have the police arriving in the middle of the night. I'm sure you understand."

"Of course," I almost whisper. Jeannine, thin, neat, dressed in standard green scrubs is consistently kind and serious. Knowing my mother is an early riser, she has often personally delivered her an early morning coffee -- before the dining room is open to residents. She cares. I trust her.

I return to Mother's room to interrogate.

"Why did you call 911 last night?" I demand.

"There was a strange man in my room rummaging through my closet. I'm not going to let anyone rob me. I know what to do, so I called for help. That's what the 911 number is for."

"Could it be that someone who works here was just putting away your laundry?" I ask, trying to make sense of this scenario.

"Then they should do that in the daytime, so they don't scare the wits out of an old woman. They shouldn't be prowling around in the dark in people's rooms."

I have to admit I agree with her, but I don't tell her that. I say, "They are probably trying to make sure the night shift is useful and has plenty to do."

"I tell you, I could run this place better than it's run now. They have too many kids working here and they aren't adequately supervised. They don't have good manners either. They need to learn to say *yes ma'am* and *no ma'am* and *yes sir* and *no sir.…*"

I am amazed at my mother's lucidity today. It's as if she woke up minus her dementia. Sometimes it's like this, and I feel sure my mother is better. Then, an hour later, she'll be rambling on about taking a trip on the train to Mexico the night before. Based on a lifetime of watching her focus her will and put her organizational skills to use, at this moment, I believe she *could* run this place. I know she's got a keen mind for managing things and figuring out creative alternatives to common problems. *Don't wait for someone else to do it for you, do it yourself* was a message oft repeated. You need to be able to take care of yourself. You may be a woman, but you can take care of yourself.

My mother didn't teach me to be a man in a man's world, she taught me to be an independent woman in what she perceived to be a man's world. Even here at the nursing home, she points out, "I went to Mr. Ricks' office." "You know he's the man who runs this place."

"The administrator," I reply.

"I don't care what they call him. He doesn't care about us. I had some suggestions for improving things, and I could tell he wasn't listening. I'm not stupid."

"What were your suggestions?"

"I told him we need shower stalls with handrails and benches in the bathrooms. And privacy, too."

"What else?"

"We should be able to sit wherever we want in the dining room. We're adults."

"Did he say what he would do with your suggestions?"

"No. That's why I know he wasn't listening. He just said thank you and sent me on my way. He could learn something, but he's not interested."

At this moment, I am proud that my mother has a voice and speaks up. She's earned it.

She loved to tell the story of her own mother challenging the age old family custom of family dinners where the women cooked, the men were served first, the children second, and the women last, eating whatever was left. "I must have been ten or eleven, 1930 or 1931. My momma just went into the dining room where all the men were seated and said, 'It's time for a change. We women are going to sit here with you men. We can all visit while the children eat at the kitchen table.' It didn't hurt that she was her daddy's favorite, the oldest child, a daddy's girl."

The goddess, Athena, daughter of Zeus, is said to have sprung from her father's brow. Known for being at ease in a man's world, she had the ability to apply her animus, the gift of logical and intuitive thinking, to create practical solutions for problems. All this, while maintaining a clear head in spite of powerful emotions surrounding her. I am trying to apply those same gifts, as a result, in this nursing home this morning as I discover my mother has called the police here three times. Now I have to remove one more thing that connects her to the life she once had -- her phone. She won't be able to just sit in a chair in her room and dial up her brother, her sister-in-law, her best friend, her son, or me.

She will have to go to the public phone in a public area and be limited in the amount of time she can talk If we want to call her, someone will have to go get her and bring her to the phone. More loss, not just for her, but for me, for all of us. I think of all the ways we communicate these days -- phone, fax, e-mail, mail... - we have many options for connecting to the world. Now, with the removal of her phone from her room, her connection to the world is diminished one more time. How much more loss can she take?

\* \* \*

"How long are you going to stand over me like that?" Mother asks.

I am unaware that, at some point, she sat down in her chair, and I remained standing. I sit down on the bed, and say, "Mother, we have to take your phone out of your room because you have been calling 911."

She stomps her feet on the floor and wails, "Nooooo.... You can't. I won't let you. Where is my phone? Give me my phone."

Athena's outrage at the injustice of lost communication is palpable in this room. I know not to rush to her side and comfort her. She will shrug me off in anger. Yet, like Athena, if she could allow me to hold her as she sobs, her body would help inform her mind. She would know

53

that this, too, shall pass. But she is in full armor now, her ego defended. I have seen her like this many times before. She's on a mission with a message and there's no stopping her. She does not want comfort. She wants action.

\* \* \*

Mother had years of practice in taking action as she organized our household moves each time my daddy changed jobs and we followed him to the new location. She collected boxes at the local grocery store, saved newspapers to wrap the precious items, went room by room labeling each box so unpacking would be easy. When we arrived, it would take her only a couple of days to have our household running smoothly again. After she had the house ship-shape, she found us a church and a school and a doctor. Then she went door to door and introduced herself to the neighbors, gathering the troops, putting her defensive/offensive strategy into place.

"It's important to know your neighbors," she said, "because you might need them and they might need you." She didn't like to "let the grass grow under her feet" as she would say. She may have mourned yet another move, but she didn't let it stop her from doing what needed to be done. *Make the best of your situation and move* on was a motto she lived by.

\* \* \*

If I wanted comfort, I went to my daddy. Mother wasn't going to "let me whine" as she put it. *Get on with your life* was her message. There's no time for sitting around and lamenting over what went wrong, *do something.*

When I broke up with the man I thought I was meant to marry, I was devastated. I thought I was going to die. I couldn't sleep or eat. I was in college, living at home in an apartment attached to my parents' house. Daddy came into my room, sat down on the bed beside me, held my hand, patted my back, and said, "Do you want to talk about it?" He listened while I told my sad story. Is it any wonder I thought of myself as a daddy's girl? We talked and planned and envisioned. Time with him was quiet and absent of huge emotions and demands. Mother came in, threw open the curtains letting light flood the room, pulled the covers off me, and declared, "Get up! It's time to stop wallowing around in your misery. There are more fish in the sea. He's not the only man in the world." As mad at her as I was, I knew she meant business. I got up.

Years later, when that same man, who I'd ended up marrying, left me after nine years and three children together, I could tell myself, after a week of wallowing, "Get up! It's time to take care of yourself and your three children." I'd learned my mother's lesson well. Athena's shield was firmly attached. I was protected and prepared.

\* \* \*

Now she is rummaging around in her closet. I don't know what she is looking for, but I am sure it would be hard to find in the crowded, jumbled mess inside that tiny space.

"Is it something you need?" I ask.

"My purse. I have to have a receipt."

She hasn't kept a receipt for years. I have been paying her bills and filing her receipts in a plastic file box for her.

"I paid for that phone," she shouts. "They can't take it away from me. *I* paid for it!"

"Yes, you paid for it," I agree. "Now they want you to *stop* paying for your own phone and use the one in the living room." I can hear Larry's voice in my head saying, *you are being rational with an irrational person*, something my mother taught me to do decades ago. I would attempt to explain my point of view to her about something she wanted me to do that I didn't want to do. "I *don't want* to be a teacher. I want to be an actress," I'd say.

"Yes, you *do want* to be a teacher. It's the practical thing."

Practicality was on the top of her list in determining what choice should be made. "A woman needs her own money, so she doesn't have to ask permission to buy something when she wants it. My grandma, Nanny Jane, always kept her egg money for her knick knacks. She didn't want to have to ask Grandpa for money."

\* \* \*

"You always made sure I knew how to make money to pay for my own things, Mother," I say. "I remember the day you took me to Gindler's Department Store to apply for a job. Do you remember that?"

"I sure do. You were as stubborn that day as you are right now. Tell them I need my phone."

\* \* \*

I am distracted by her accusing me of being stubborn on that summer day in 1961 when she demanded that I go into Gindler's and apply for a part-time job - Saturdays and after school during the week. I had never seen a person under the age of my parents working there, plus they didn't have a Help Wanted sign anywhere. I told her as much. She replied, planted in front of the store windows, hands on her hips, "We'll stay out here in front of this store as long as it takes for you to go in there and ask for a job." Who was she calling stubborn? I knew she meant business. I went in and asked for a job while she waited on the sidewalk outside. Hands perspiring, heart beating, I went straight to Mr. Johnson, who, she had told me, was the manager. It was easy to find him because he was the only man in the store. "Mr. Johnson, my name is Beverly Brothers," I said to him. I will be a senior at the high school this fall, and I was wondering if you need anyone to work after school and on Saturdays. I love Gindler's and would like to work here."

He was trim and neat, bald on top with a ring of black hair around the edge of the bald spot. He wore a white shirt and blue striped tie. Kind and business-like in his demeanor, he made me comfortable. "Do you know how to operate a cash register and make change?" he asked.

"I can make change, and if someone will teach me how to use the cash register, I am sure I can do it."

"Let's take a moment and see how quick you are on the cash register."

I listened carefully as he instructed, and then I did what he had taught me. He had me fill out some papers so I could be paid. "Can you be here to work next Saturday from 8:00 a.m. to 6:00 p.m.?"

"Yes, sir. Thank you so much."

I returned to the sidewalk where my mother was waiting patiently. "Did you get a
job?" she asked.

"I got a job – Saturdays from eight to six and every day after school from four to six."

"How much will you make?"

"I receive a 10% discount on merchandise, and I'll get paid fifty cents an hour."

"See? I told you so. You have to ask for what you want. You can't sit around and wait for it to come to you. Go after it. God helps those who help themselves."

"It wasn't that easy. I had to pass a cash register test and fill out a bunch of papers," I replied. *How dare she assume it was just about going in and asking for it, I thought?*

I loved that job and I discovered I had a talent for sales, something I never told my mother.

It was my senior year in high school, and I was also taking an elective called secretarial training. "Not," my mother said, "so you can be a secretary, but so that you can use those skills to get a job to help pay your way through college so you can have a degree in education and teach. You'll be a teacher."

I wanted to be an actress on Broadway or in film. I had expressed that desire periodically since I was four and taking expression and dance lessons from my Aunt Benelle; each time I did, my mother replied, "No, you want to be a teacher."

Like Athena, my momma was tireless, practical, persevering, and single-minded in directing me down a career path she had, most likely, dreamed of for herself. How many times had I heard her say, "I would have been a good teacher?" Now she was determined I'd fulfill that dream. "You can't depend on making your own living as an actress. That's too chancy. Teaching is something you can always fall back on. It's a respectable profession with a decent salary."

At the time these conversations were taking place, there were basically two professions open to women - teaching and nursing. I shivered at the sight of blood and vomit, so it was clear to her, I guess, that my profession would be teacher. Like Athena, she was ensuring that I would be protected from the peril of poverty and that I would be respected for the work I was doing. She had no concept of my *being called* to something different than what she had chosen for me.

By the time I was six, I was already a fan of the stage and screen, something I'd learned at my first recital. When those thick maroon velvet curtains were drawn, the lights went up, and I tapped my way out on stage, I trembled with delight, not fear. The tune was "That's Peggy O'Neill," and in my green and white checked bloomers and midriff baring top, I sang and danced my heart out. It didn't matter that the stage was in a building that doubled as a gymnasium for high school basketball games. Later in the evening, I put on a ruffled evening dress and showed my expression and memorization skills in a piece called "Taking 'Spression Lessons." The applause was heady.

When Vera Ellen, Monte Hale, Gabby Hayes, and Gene Autry came to our little town in the '50's, I was in the front row to see them. I had pestered my mother to take me. Here they were in flesh and blood, the Saturday afternoon matinee entertainers I had seen on the screen at the local picture show. I just wished they had brought Cyd Charisse and Esther Williams along. The elaborate musicals, synchronized swimming, and thrilling westerns made for hours of entertainment. My brother, our friends, cousins, and I reenacted scenes from shows we had seen or we made up our own - complete with costumes, blankets for stage curtains, and popcorn in waxtex bags for our audience members.

\* \* \*

"Beverly Ann. Beverly Ann," Mother says, nudging my arm. "*Where in the world did you go?* I've been talking and you haven't even been listening. Did you hear me?"

Dust motes are floating in the light from the window. I notice the ivy has three dead

leaves. I need to pluck those, I think to myself.

"I was just thinking about my job at Gindler's and how you made me apply even when I didn't want to."

"And it was a good job, wasn't it?"

"It sure was."

"I don't even know what your job is now. When people ask, I can't even explain it. 'What's a consultant?' they say. 'What does she consult on?' I just wish you'd kept on teaching."

"I know," I tell her. I have had my own business for twenty years and she is still mourning my career change. "Why did you consent to dancing and expression lessons and all that make believe when I was growing up? It didn't seem to me like you approved of it."

"That's kid stuff. Kids need to play. Grown-ups have to work. You're a lot like your daddy. He was a dreamer, too. I wanted to make sure you could make a life for yourself - that you didn't need someone to take care of you."

I want to put my hands over my ears like I did as a child. Instead, I pluck the three dead leaves from the plant on the bedside table, throw them in the trash, and pick up her suitcase.

* * *

Before leaving the nursing home with my mother, I have called the phone company to cancel service, and I have asked the nurse to dispose of her white touch tone - - chosen for décor reasons. I packed her bag for the weekend trip as well.

"Mother, look at the bluebonnets and Indian Paintbrushes. You'll enjoy this ride," I say as we head south on highway 77A.

"They're sure pretty," she replies. We've had enough rain this year, so there should be a lot of wildflowers."

"I remember springs by the Easter dresses you sewed for me," I tell her. Driving her through the country on roads so familiar to both of us, I ask, "Do you remember all those Easter dresses?"

She bites into her small vanilla custard, a treat from the Dairy Queen. When she doesn't respond, I think of the nursing home social worker's advice, "It's better for you to remember *for her* than to ask her to remember."

I describe two of my favorite dresses aloud. "I was six when you made the red and white dotted swiss with red ribbon threaded between each tier of the skirt and around the yoke. I had a broad-brimmed straw hat that you trimmed with the same red ribbon. You were such a creative seamstress."

When there is no response, I say, "We'll look at the pictures in the scrapbook when we get to my house."

* * *

*My scrapbook has two entire pages of the black and white photographs of that Easter morning. My younger brother, Bobby, dressed in a snowy white suit and I stand side by side squinting into the sun. We look posed and our Easter baskets are brimming. We are both perfectly coiffed and ready for Sunday School. It is 1951 and America is full of dreams and we hold the promise of the dreams our parents long to fulfill -- pretty children raised in a Christian home, pretty new three-bedroom house, Easter baskets full of eggs.*

I continue, "I was in fourth grade when you made me that yellow waffle pique sundress with matching bolero. Gold rickrack glistened from the neck of the sundress and all around the bolero's edge. On a shopping trip to Victoria, I picked out white mesh Mary Janes trimmed with navy blue leather. You and Daddy tried to talk me out of them. Finally you said, 'They're pretty shoes, even if they'll be hard to polish.'"

"Can we stop for a drink? I'm thirsty. There's a Stop 'n Go. Pull in there," Mother directs me.

"I'll pull in at the Sonic," I reply.

I can't leave her in the car alone anymore. I tried it last week, and in less than five minutes, a stranger was bringing her in and inquiring if she "belonged" to anyone in the store. He said he'd found her in the parking lot.

* * *

I am thinking of three lessons I learned while wearing that yellow pique dress. One -- she told me that I couldn't take the bolero off in church because *sundresses weren't proper attire in church.* The tone of her voice told me not to argue. Two -- I was wearing that dress when she marched from where she was sitting with Daddy in the back pew of the First Baptist Church to the front pew where I was sitting with the children's choir. She took my arm and marched me up the aisle and out the door where I was swatted twice and told, *"Don't ever sit in church and play like you are some floozy."* What were you thinking?" I had been rolling up Juicy Fruit gum papers and making pretend cigarettes for me and my fellow choristers who were joining me in "smoking" vigorously in our front row seats. Three -- I was wearing that dress at school one day when a funeral procession came by on the way to the cemetery. We were at recess on the playground and every child and teacher knelt down as the cars, with headlights glowing, moved down the narrow road. After they passed, we arose in unison and continued our play. On the first day of school we had been told, "If you are outside when a funeral procession goes by, *kneel as a symbol of respect for the dead and the grieving*. It is the civilized thing to do."

Mother was my strictest civilizer. Robert Johnson, a Jungian therapist, says that *we each have civilizers*, usually our parents, who teach and guide and set parameters for us. Athena is the goddess of civilization. To live in community, one must be civilized.

As a teenager, wanting a break from my civilizer, I looked for the signs of *do as I say, not as I do*. I remember how money was tight by the time I was in high school. My two best friends, Barbara and Bobbie, had *ready-made* clothes from stores in a Houston mall they frequented. The Easter of my freshman year, Mother made me a lime green dotted swiss dress with an empire waist and a white collar and cuffs. I never felt pretty in that dress. It reminded me of curtains. I had my first pair of heels. They pinched when I walked, and I knew I could never wear them again. When we got home from church Mother rubbed shortening on the soles and shined them up so they looked brand new. "We'll go in this week and exchange them for a pair of flats," she told me.

"I don't want to. They'll know I've worn them," I told her. After all, hadn't she herself taught me white lies were wrong? Now, she was letting the practical thing to do rule out over the right thing to do.

"Don't argue with me," she said.

We exchanged the shoes. I was grateful for the new shoes that didn't hurt, but I didn't tell her.

\* \* \*

I hear a slurping sound -- the cup is empty and she is attempting to get the last drop. In her former life, prior to dementia, I think, she would never have done that. "I agree with your daddy, that sound is rude," she'd chide when Bobby or I slurped. "It sounds desperate, like you don't know where your next drink is coming from. Where are your manners?"

"Sounds like you reached the bottom of that cup," I say. "Let me toss it in the trash for you, and we'll head on down the road. Larry's expecting us."

She falls asleep, and the hum of the road is my only company. I miss her telling me stories as we drive past our old house in Yoakum, cross the Guadalupe River, pass a country dance hall.

When we arrive in Port Aransas, Larry greets us in the driveway, hugging us both and taking Mother's suitcase from me. "Hey, Charlyne. I thought we'd fight over who makes the best potato salad. I made up a bowl, using my favorite recipe -- no pimentos."

She doesn't answer. That's so unlike her. Typically, she'd reply, "It's not potato salad without pimentos," and they'd banter.

Larry tries again. "Charlyne, let's eat lunch and then go to the beach to feed the seagulls."

She is halfway up the steps, holding on tight to the deck handrail. "Help me," she pleads. Her fear is palpable. "Someone help me."

I go to her side, take her arm, and assist her in climbing the last three steps. Inside, she collapses on the sofa. "I'm so tired."

"I'll bring you a plate of food," I offer. "You can eat right here at the coffee table."

"No. I want to come to the table. Just give me a minute."

It is only Friday. I have planned for her to stay until Monday. I am already weary.

* * *

How can I say that? She has been there for me repeatedly throughout my life.

In 1971, my youngest daughter, Brooke, was born with spinabifida myelomeningocele, and was in neo-natal intensive care for three weeks. My husband and I were both teachers. We had a four-year-old son, Jeff, and an eleven-month-old daughter, Whitney. Our health insurance was an 80/20 policy. That twenty percent of the medical expenses we incurred was a lot of money from our combined incomes. In fact, our old refrigerator had stopped working a week after Brooke's birth and we could not afford to buy a new one. Overcoming our pride, we had to rely on the generosity of my Sunday School teacher who loaned us the extra one in her garage until "you can afford to buy one." I needed to work, and I was torn between that need and my concern about who would care for my children. Mother and I talked on the phone.

"We bring Brooke home tomorrow," I say. "I report to work in one week, and I still haven't found just the right person to come to the house to be with the kids."

"It will work out," my mother told me. "Didn't you get a recommendation from Kay that you thought looked good?"

"I interviewed her, but she's not available until January. Barbara gave me the name of someone else to call. Maybe I should just quit my job and stay home with the kids."

"No way. You just got that job in a great school district. You can't quit."

"I can't leave my three kids with just anyone," my voice breaks into sobs. "My kids need their mom right now. I shouldn't be leaving them."

"Crying won't help," she admonishes. "Your kids can have a mom *and* you can have a job. Calm down and *think* this through. I'll think about it myself and call you in the morning."

The next morning she called. "Your daddy and I have talked and I will come on Monday mornings early and leave on Friday afternoons for as long as you need me there. We live close enough so it isn't a big problem for us."

"You hate driving on the freeway and finding your way around in San Antonio."

"Don't argue. I can learn to do it."

I didn't argue. It did work for a semester. She helped me hold the space to create this new life with its new responsibilities.

Years later when I was a single mom and wanted to go to a weekend prayer retreat at Laity Lodge, she volunteered to come stay with the kids. I arrived home on Sunday afternoon, wanting to tell her all about the experience. She said, "I've got to go. I don't want to drive home in the dark." She left. I was angry with her, feeling discounted and unloved. Then I noticed the pie she'd baked, the laundry she'd done, the dusted bookshelves, and the supper waiting. I had a huge *ah ha*. She *did* things to show me her love. She may not have wanted to listen to my retreat experiences or discuss our spiritual journeys together, but she was there for me, doing the practical things that needed to be done.

Like Athena, she was the master of destiny, counseling me to engage in all that would offer me a deeply satisfying life while teaching me that caring for the practical and domestic needs was a vital part of that life.

When she retired at age seventy-eight after forty years as a childcare provider, she had managed to pay off the house she'd badgered Daddy into making a down payment on, save a "nest egg" as she called it, and had been taking care of her own needs for the twenty-two years since she'd been widowed. She sold her house and bought a smaller one so she could have the difference to enhance her social security and allow her to retire. She was determined to take care of herself. Now, not being able to do so any longer was an unbearable grief.

\* \* \*

Mother's "minute" on the sofa has passed and she has joined us at the kitchen table. "Do you want a slice of ham with your potato salad?" Larry asks.

"I sure do. Do you have any pickles?" she replies.

The three of us are finally ready to enjoy our very late lunch. It is Good Friday and I mention that before we bless our food.

"We Protestants never did much on Good Friday. That was more of a Catholic event," she says. "Our town was really divided. Protestants didn't marry Catholics. They didn't even date them," she continues. "I didn't want you to have the stress of a mixed marriage. It's just easier when you both have the same beliefs."

\* \* \*

"Southern Baptists aren't Protestants," I would have said to her in the past, "and is there any marriage where both people have the same beliefs?"

Then she would have said, "You know I was raised a Methodist," in a tone that let me know she didn't want to be challenged. "I just joined the Baptist church 'cause your daddy wouldn't join the Methodist and you and Bobby needed to have a church home. I don't believe like those Baptists. They believe once saved always saved. That kind of belief just allows them to do whatever they want and repent on their death beds. Methodists fall from grace. That makes more sense to me."

I have been reading a book of Lenten meditations during this season, and recall how Lent was never even part of my vocabulary while growing up. In our Southern Baptist world, the resurrection was the highlight of

Easter. Christ may have died for our sins, but we skipped on as quickly as possible to choruses of "Up from the grave He arose..."

\* \* \*

Later that afternoon, two local friends, Gene and Margaret, both of whom had been active in my campaign for City Council last year, stop by to deliver some cookies and an Easter card. I introduce my mother to them and Gene says, "I bet you are really proud of your daughter. She ran a winning campaign, and she's doing a good job on the Council."

She has been slumped into the arm of the sofa, and she straightens herself up and replies, "I didn't raise my daughter to be a politician. I raised her to be a teacher."

I am surprised by her response, and embarrassed. It has a challenging sound, and it is clear from Gene's response that he doesn't know what to say.

\* \* \*

Truth be known, she *did* raise me to be a politician. Hopefully, in the finest sense of the word. A politician must have a voice -- be a voice for the people she serves. Councilmen are elected to ensure that the community is financially sound and physically safe, and that the city charter is honored. There are layers to those responsibilities. Complexity is part of the job. Reading, studying, researching, and listening to the many and varied voices of the community is essential. Making decisions with regard for both the individual and the whole community requires both courage and discernment. It requires the wisdom of Athena, the wise old owl.

Athena's association with cities and her "cheerleading" for various heroes led Odysseus to say of her, "She always stands beside me in all my tasks and always remembers me wherever I go." Athena always meets us when we need her most. She infuses us with courage. When we take on challenges, encounter obstacles, or find ourselves overcome with doubt, she is at our side, the warrior woman reminding us, "You have all you need to succeed. Be brave and move forward."

Mother was a warrior woman. So many of her life's actions and choices reflected this Athena spirit. I recall that even the hymns my parents declared as their favorites were indicative of the roles they had chosen to play in my life.

Once a month on Sunday evening at First Baptist Church we had a hymn sing. We were invited to raise our hand, be recognized by the song leader, shout out the hymn page number, and the congregation would join in singing the song of our choice.

My daddy would call out page 428 in the Baptist Hymnal, his favorite, "In the Garden," a love song for God and us. The first verse and chorus said, "*I go to the garden alone while the dew is still on the roses and the voice I hear falling on my ear, the Son of God discloses. And He walks with me and He talks with me, and He tells me I am His own, and the joy we share as we tarry there, none other has ever known.*"

In contrast, my mother asked for page 400, "No, Never Alone", a song that made me think of God protecting us in battle. "*I've seen the lightning flashing, I've heard the thunder roll. I've felt sin's breakers dashing, trying to conquer my soul. I've heard the voice of Jesus telling me still to fight on. He promised never to leave me, never to leave me alone. No, never alone, no, never alone….*"

Singing Daddy's song made me feel peaceful, surrounded by beauty, related to God, and singing Mother's song made me feel vigilant, courageous, protected by God. It would be years before I recognized these were gifts they bequeathed to me.

Daddy measured out his words like he did the sugar for his iced tea on a summer evening. He philosophized, giving words emphasis when he wanted you to remember them. I have his "sermons" stored deep inside, ready for retrieval in times of need. His words encouraged, affirmed, gave solace.

Mother's words poured out from some endless supply stored inside waiting to spill forth at all times. She directed, using words to prepare you for life's vicissitudes. I have her directions readily available, moving me forward even in times of distress. Her words challenged, confronted, instructed.

\* \* \*

Now I'd found I needed both of these teachers as I navigated the life I was currently living. My election to City Council came just two months before my mother's move into the nursing home. I wondered if

I could serve my hometown well, care for my mother's increasing needs, be the wife Larry deserved, be the kind of mother and grandmother I wanted to be, and continue working in the business I had started twenty years before.

"Live to your full potential," was a mantra I'd chanted to my own three children. It was the legacy of being my mother's daughter. This is the Athena in my mother talking.

I had that message in my DNA, so the answer to whether or not I could handle all of the above was a resounding *yes.*

\* \* \*

Speaking of my mother's voice, I hear her say, "Are those people gone?"

She had dozed off on the couch as Larry and I visited with our friends. I hadn't waked her when they left.

"Yes, they said to tell you they were glad to meet you," I tell her.

"What time is it?" she inquires. Her hair is mussed after her nap on the sofa, and she is a little groggy.

"It's almost six o'clock."

"Did I miss the news?"

"We missed the local news, but we can catch the national."

She always watches the news. For as long as I can remember she has wanted to know what is going on in the world, and has wanted to express her opinion about it. *And she says she didn't raise me to be a politician! Ha!*

She taught with story and example.

\* \* \*

It is the summer of 1950 and I am five. We are standing in line to buy movie tickets at the local theater. There are two lines of people buying tickets, one line has a sign that says Whites, and the other line has a sign that says Coloreds.

"I never have understood this," she says. Not really to me, more like thinking out loud. "I've always wondered why Nora can cook our hamburgers at the Confectionary, but if she wants a hamburger at any café in town, she has to go to the back door to buy it."

I know Nora because she helps my grandma cook and clean sometimes, especially if there's going to be a lot of people at Grandma's house. Sometimes Grandma and Nora sit on the back porch in the swing and gossip while Nora dips snuff. I like to listen.

"Could Nora sit with us in the movie?" I ask.

"No, she couldn't." She looks around to see who might be listening, then adds, "That's a disgrace."

\* \* \*

During a December cold spell last year, Mother and I were taking an afternoon drive through the country, a respite from the monotony of the nursing home. I'd passed a vacant lot on the edge of town. Weeds as tall as a man covered the lot.

Pointing to the lot, Mother said, "That was where the Negro school used to be. I don't see how they stood it on a cold day like this one. There were cracks in the walls so big you could put your hand through them. Why do you think they put up with that?"

It is just weeks from Martin Luther King, Jr. Day.

"Remember Martin Luther King, Jr?" I ask. "He wouldn't tolerate separate lines for blacks and whites or segregated schools, so he took a stand."

"I remember the riots. I just can't get used to calling Negroes blacks," she responds. "It just doesn't sound respectful."

\* \* \*

The Easter weekend is over. It is Monday morning, and I am driving my mother back to the nursing home. We left early to avoid the after-holiday ferry traffic which can result in an hour and a half wait. We are an hour out of Port Aransas when she says, "I don't have my cosmetic bag. It has my medicines in it. Go back. I have to have my medicines."

I pull to the shoulder of the road. My stomach is churning. I feel anger enveloping me. *How* could she have forgotten her medicines? NO, how could *I* have forgotten her medicines? I am filled with the paradox of where to focus this anger which has invaded my body.

"Why didn't you put them in your suitcase?" I ask her. "I put your medicines on the kitchen table and told you to put them in your suitcase."

"Don't be mad at me. You know I'm forgetful. You need to help me remember."

"I *did* help you remember. I put them in front of you and told you to put them in your suitcase. The nursing home makes me sign to take your medicines with me and sign in when I bring them back. Are you sure you didn't pack them?"

What am I doing talking to my mother this way? My mother has dementia. She is not the "can do, take charge" mother of my past. This is a new mother. This mother needs *my* help. Still, I am not ready to lose the "can do, take charge" mother. I am angry because that mother is leaving me all alone to take care of not just myself, but now her also.

I start crying. She starts crying. We are sitting on the side of the road, two warrior women bound by our tears.

Then she starts laughing. "This is an adventure," she says. "We are having an adventure."

Adventures are what we have always called mishaps or things gone wrong. Somehow it helps shift our perspective.

"Yes, we are having an adventure," I repeat her words. "We'll turn around and go back to get your medications. Now we've got a story to tell - - a story of our adventure."

\* \* \*

Driving, I recall what my friend, Sue, said to me over coffee a few days after my daughter, Whitney's, wedding. "After hearing 'Charlyne' stories from you all these years, I have to admit I was surprised when I met your mother in person. She's so small. I bet she's no more than five foot three. I pictured her being much taller."

"I take after my daddy's side of the family where the women were tall," I explain. "On my mother's side, the women were short. Her mother was only four foot eleven."

"I'm not talking about size," Sue says. "It's just that all your stories make her seem so big and powerful, so strong and confrontational. Then I meet this little, friendly, white haired woman who is so polite and nice."

In my mind, I hear the stories I have told through the years, the stories that have captured my imagination and helped shape and inform my life.

I remember seeing Woody Allen's movie, *Life Lessons*, where the mother loomed like a gigantic balloon over the city. I resonated with that image. That's the way I saw my mother. Years later, when reading a book by Thomas Moore, I wrote a quotation in my journal that helped me understand my perception a little more -- "*Fact is an illusion, because every fact is part of a story and is riddled with imagination. Imagination is real because every perception of the world around us is absolutely colored by the narrative or image-filled lens through which we perceive. We are all poets and artists as we live our daily lives, whether or not we recognize this role and whether or not we believe it.*" I want to believe it.

My imagination has brought the goddesses here to be with my mother and me as we traverse the trails of dementia. I am grateful for Athena and her gifts of practical thinking, courage, and intuitive wisdom. My mother is bigger than life to me. I need help in understanding her. But first things first.

* * *

Right now I'm on the side of the road. I need to use my Athena thinking to decide how to make a U-Turn and head back to the house to find my mother's medicine. They won't let her back in the nursing home without it.

# CHAPTER FIVE

## OBSESSION

## DEMETER

## GODDESS OF MOTHERHOOD, FERTILITY, AND HARVEST

*"…we're connecting, foot under my rib.*
*I'm sore with life."*
- from *Poems for the New*, Kathleen Fraser,
poet and co-founder of feminist poetics newsletter, HOW(ever)

*Painting by Miriana Ilieva*
*Daughter-in-law, Granddaughter-in-law*

Year Three

# Obsession

It is night, and I have come home from a day-long trip in which I returned my mother to her nursing home – complete with her medications. After several trips, I have learned my lesson about those medications. Though I am exhausted from driving six hours, sitting in the ferry lines,, and helping settle my mother back into her routine, I cannot sleep.

In my study now, I face a print of a painting by Meinrad Craighead named Mother Daughter. Two magnificent females face each other, braided hair entwined, arms circling one another, surrounded by wheat and flowers, each anointed by a sliver of silver moon. A lush, ripened pomegranate sits in the circle above their breasts. For most people, Demeter is thought of in relationship to her daughter, Persephone, so strong is their bond. On Mt. Olympus, Demeter's most important roles were mother and provider of food and spiritual sustenance. The need to nurture, nourish, heal, and give generously is illustrated in the story of Demeter.

I bought this print in 1997 at a time when I was being called to my mother's aid on a regular basis, even though I lived a significant distance away. I had moved for several reasons, one of which was to escape the hold of my mother. Who was I fooling? Miles, I discovered, could not sever the ties of my relationship with her.

The phone rings, breaking the silence, interrupting my thoughts. It is midnight. *Who would be calling at this hour*, I think? I grab the phone, hoping it hasn't wakened Larry who went to sleep hours ago.

"Hello," I whisper.

"This is Melody at Comfort Care. I'm sorry to disturb you, but I need to let you know your mother has had an accident."

My heart beats faster. I am on alert, geared to take action. "What kind of accident?"

"She fell and tumbled over the front of her walker. She landed on her face, so it's bruised. We took her to the emergency room. She had to have four stitches in her forehead, and now she's asleep in her room."

73

"Asleep in her room, where? The hospital? The nursing home?" I ask.

"Here, at the nursing home," Melody replies.

Her name implies song, musical harmony, and her voice belies that meaning. She is methodical and emotionless. She's talking about my mother falling, cutting her head open, and going to the emergency room as if it were the most everyday thing in the world. I feel both my fury and my lifelong desire to care for my mother rising up in me.

"How did this happen?"

I want an explanation. After all, I have just spent the last months making changes in her living arrangements, based on recommendations from medical professionals, and her situation continues to deteriorate. Now what do I do? Do I run to her in the middle of the night to see if she's really okay? Do I trust that Melody is telling me the truth about Mother already being asleep after her mishap? Do I do what I have always done – struggle with whether her needs are real or imagined ones? Mother had always found a way to get my attention, after all.

Melody's voice interrupts my thinking. "We don't know how it happened. No one saw her fall."

I want to scream accusations, but instead, I say, "I don't know whether to come now or wait until morning."

"No need to come now. I told you she's asleep. It's our policy to let a family member know when a resident has to go to the hospital."

I want to believe her, this Melody. I'm just not sure I can. I am my mother's designated care giver. Of course, she's in the nursing home and they ensure her basic needs are met, but I am the one who cares *about* her. She is my mother, my Demeter. At the core of Demeter's being is her abundant love. She is a nurturer, a caretaker, a healer. She's motivated by the most powerful of instincts – to give life. She devotes herself to the life she creates. Carl Jung said, *"Every mother contains her daughter in herself, and every daughter her mother, and every woman extends backwards into her mother and forwards into her daughter."* Like my mother, I at times become entrapped by my desire to mother. When that happens, I have to step back, discern when it is time to say no to the needs of others, establish my boundaries, and put myself first. This is one of those times. Can I do it?

\* \* \*

Months before Mother's fall, I'd arrived at her former care facility to find her dazed and dirty. She was lying on her bed in a white cotton turtleneck shirt that didn't belong to her, and a pair of elastic-waisted pants that, in the past, she would have worn only to do her gardening. The shirt had food stains on it. When I inquired about her attire for our day out together, she didn't reply. She appeared sleepy. I put clean clothes on her and brushed her hair. It felt as though I were dressing a rag doll. Determined to have her wake up and enjoy a day out, I coaxed her to the car and we proceeded to drive to my brother's house for a visit. She slept the entire way. We had an abbreviated version of the visit I had anticipated. I knew something was wrong, so we returned to the nursing home early.

Upon our arrival, I helped my mother into her bed and went straight to the nurses' station.

"Something's wrong with my mother. She can't wake up," I said to the woman at the desk, someone I did not recognize.

"What room is she in? I'll finish this, and then come down there to take her vitals," she replied as she kept writing on the paper in front of her.

"What is your name?" I demanded.

Looking up from her paper, she said, "Jolene." Tension filled the air between us. She was angry about being interrupted, and I was angry that she wasn't taking my request seriously.

"How long have you worked here, Jolene?" I asked.

"I fill in when they need me," she said.

"I don't know who the 'they' is," I snipped, "but my mother needs you. Now!"

I felt like Shirley MacLaine in *Terms of Endearment* – the scene where she stands at the nurses' station screaming, "Give my daughter her medication! Give my daughter her medication!"

Jolene and I walked to my mother's room. She was asleep. Jolene took her temperature, blood pressure, and announced, "Her blood pressure is lower than normal, *but* she's asleep."

"She's been asleep ALL DAY! That's *not* normal. I want you to call the doctor."

"It's Sunday night," she replied.

"Does that mean you don't call the doctor on Sunday night?" I inquired.

Jolene glared at me. I glared back. I noticed her stance, tightly permed coiffure, small eyes, no accessories, the stethoscope around her neck, starched clothes, absence of affect. I deduced that I was gazing on a serious, stubborn person.

"I only call the doctor if it's an emergency," she stated.

"I'll call the doctor myself," I said.

Dr. Robinson was on call. He listened and told me to bring my mother to the emergency room where she was diagnosed with severe dehydration. I learned, at this time, that the elderly are prone to dehydration which can lead to death. She was in the hospital for two days and nights. Her dementia escalated during this brief hospital stay. I left to shower and change clothes, and returned to find her strapped into a geriatric chair at the nurses' station. She had been taking out her IV and trying to leave. I was informed that I needed to stay in the hospital 24/7, hire someone to stay, or have Mother experience the degradation of being strapped into a gerry chair while she struggled to release herself from an obviously unendurable confinement.

I received a gentle reminder, at the time, from Dr. Robinson who told me that my mother would only continue to decline and that one day "she won't even recognize you." In spite of his warning, I thought to myself – how could this be true? How could my mother be out of her mind? I was repeating a pattern in my mother's and my relationship that was similar to Demeter and Persephone's - I was resisting meeting the dark mother, the one who leaves me with deep emptiness, a feeling of being shunned, and left behind. No action I can take will change this mother, yet I keep taking action, hoping for a different response. There's an old saying that *if you keep on doing what you've always done, you'll keep on getting what you've always gotten*. Do I really believe I can change my mother's condition?

I needed someone to blame. Obviously it was the nursing home at fault, the nursing home that had caused my mother's present difficulty. I made arrangements to move her to Comfort Care, a facility in the same town. The move was traumatic for her and for me.

Yet, she had been at the new facility less than a week, and I received a call from the administrator, Emily.

"Beverly, your mom is leaving the building," she told me. "Since we are on a highway, it is a dangerous situation. We would like to put a sensor on her ankle so we'll hear an alarm when she exits the building. Is that okay with you?"

Emily impressed me from our first meeting. When my mother and I entered her office, she stood up, came toward us, smiling, and introduced herself. She radiated warmth and professionalism. Her office was a combination of work-station and living room. She explained the policies and procedures, rules and regulations in laymen's terms. She wore bright- colored suits, red, yellow, and green. When she walked through the halls, she called residents and employees by name. I was reassured that my mother's humanity would be in good hands here, with Emily at the helm.

I tried to bring these opposites together in my mind – my mother's humanity and my mother's "guard bracelet."

After some discussion, I agreed to the sensor.

Within weeks, I was agreeing to my mother's move into the Sunset Unit, a euphemism for the secured unit, the lock-down. I had to memorize a code to exit once I'd entered to visit. This was the most difficult decision I'd had to make so far. I asked for my brother's help. He attended the staff meeting with me. Wherein, they explained the unit, the reasons it was best for my mother, and ended with a tour of the area. The realization of the extent of her mental decline hit me and I wept.

My brother reassured me saying, "She'll be less stimulated in this smaller area. It's quieter here." I wanted to believe him.

I looked at the small courtyard outside the glass door. Trees, shrubs, and flowers surrounded a small gazebo with benches. I attempted to imagine mother could stay connected to Mother Earth in this small patch of garden.

\* \* \*

I don't know how long I've been sitting here since I hung up with Melody, but the question of whether to go to my mother now or stay home and go in the morning is heavy on my mind.

\* \* \*

As I lie on the couch looking at the print, my thoughts drift. It is now 1:00 in the morning. I recall vividly my parents cutting down trees and stacking branches, clearing the land to make space for the new house they are building. It is summertime and I am cold. I must be four or five.

"Momma, momma," I say, tugging at the skirt of her gingham checked housedress. "I'm cold."

"Cold!" It's ninety degrees outside. You're just bored. Go entertain yourself."

I walk to the car, crawl into the back seat, and lie down. It is almost dark. I don't know how much time has passed when I hear Momma and Daddy putting the tools in the trunk. Bobby scoots in beside me. "You're hot," he tells me.

Daddy reaches in to touch my forehead. "She has a fever," he says.

Mother moves into high gear. She picks me up, cradles me, and says, "Eddie, let's go see Dr. Dennis," using the first name of our family physician. He resides in the town where many generations of my maternal family had been born. His father delivered my mother. We drive seventeen miles to my grandma's house.

"Charlie," she tells my grandpa, "you go up to Dennis' house and tell him to come over right now."

Within minutes, Dr. Dennis is examining me as I lie in my grandparents' double bed. I am burning up with fever. "She has polio," he announces. "I'm going to let the fever burn. One of you must stay awake and watch over her to see that she doesn't convulse. I think it's the best thing to do."

Daddy pulls a chair up beside the bed. He will take the first shift. Sometime during the night, Momma comes in and relieves him. She holds my hand and whispers, "Baby, I'm right here. Momma's right here." I doze off and on.

I awake with some paralysis on my right side. Dr. Dennis makes arrangements for me to go to Warm Springs in Ottine, Texas. Momma goes with me. The rehabilitation people there teach her all the exercises that I must do to regain my strength. When we return home, she sets up a rehab station in our dining room and becomes my physical therapist for months on end. When I am able to walk and run and play again, I complain of having to wear corrective shoes.

"You're lucky to walk. I'm going to take you to see Beth Short. Then you'll appreciate your situation."

She drives me to the Shorts. On the way she tells me, "Beth was a senior in high school, drum major in the band, elected most beautiful in the school, engaged to the high school football star, and planning a wedding for the June following graduation. Now she's in an iron lung. It breathes for her, and she draws pictures with brushes her mother places in her mouth. Her fiancé is dating someone else," my momma says, as if I would understand the gravity of this information.

When I walk into her room, I am terrified. Beth Short is a head in a bullet. This is the way I would describe it. Momma walks over to her, touches her forehead, and says, "Beth, remember Beverly Ann? She's recovering from polio. I wanted her to meet you."

I hang back so Momma comes and pulls me forward to stand right by the iron lung. I can hear the laboring sound it makes. I can see Beth's pale face. I remember her prancing in front of the band in the annual Tom-Tom Parade. I know I will wear my corrective shoes as long as Momma tells me to, and I am sure that Momma's healing powers are responsible for my standing here now.

\* \* \*

One-thirty a.m. – I find my journal and try to make sense of my thoughts. *Which mother is speaking to me now – the internal or external mother?* Of course, it's the internal mother. The external one is asleep one hundred forty miles away and has been diagnosed with dementia. However, as Clarissa Pinkola Estes says in *Women Who Run With the Wolves,* "*For most adults, if there was trouble with the mother once but there is no more, there is still a duplicate mother in the psyche who sounds, acts, responds the same as in early childhood. Even though a woman's culture may have evolved into more conscious reasoning about the role of mothers, the internal mother will have the same values and ideas about what a mother should look like, act like, as those in one's childhood culture.*"

Estes tells the story of the ugly duckling and says it illustrates three mothering structures – an ambivalent mother, a collapsed mother, and an unmothered mother. The ambivalent mother is motivated by her instincts, taunted for having a child who is different, she is divided between cultural expectations and maternal love. The collapsed mother has lost her sense of self and has slid into confusion, isolation, or martyrdom. The unmothered mother who has, herself, been born to a fragile or unmothered mother does not have the resources to draw on to mother a child. Like the mother in the ugly duckling story, my mother exhibited all three.

Intellectually, I know it's insane to leave here at two a.m. and drive one hundred and forty miles, to arrive at the nursing home at five-thirty in the morning. *But*, in my gut, I'm struggling with the little girl who wants her momma's love. The same little girl who just can't obey Momma's messages all the time – the mother who says you better mind me, don't defy me, finish what you start. When I was a child and didn't mind her, she spanked me with a hairbrush, her hand, a switch off the tree, a belt, whatever was within reach when her fury overcame her rational thinking. From an early age, I stood face to face, eye to eye, with her, daring her to make me cry. She would tell me how the spanking hurt her more than me, and I would withdraw from her, laughing at the ridiculousness of such a statement. She would be enraged by my response.

I close my journal, sit, and remember.

\* \*

My mother had a lot of rules for me. I wrote an essay once called "My Momma Said." It was filled with her adages – have faith in God because we're always being tested and our task is to meet the challenge, pretty is as pretty does so mind your manners and don't talk so loud, beauty is only skin deep so have a purpose to live for, birds of a feather flock together so pay attention to the company you keep, a watched pot never boils so develop some patience…. I wanted her to approve of me, but I was always breaking one of my mother's rules.

One of the first times I recall doing so, I was six years old and had been told not to wear my ballet slippers to school, not to play with Little Polly, not to wear a dress without a slip, and never to disappear without telling her where I was. I did all four things in one day.

I hid my soft pink ballet slippers in my lunch sack and put them on in the cloakroom when I got to school. I removed them before I left school, bringing them home in my book satchel. I managed that without being caught.

On the way home from school that afternoon, Little Polly, who lived with her divorced momma, Big Polly, in a garage apartment, asked if I could come play at her house. The invitation was too exotic to refuse – a garage apartment, up the stairs, with no adult at home (her momma worked). That required some figuring out. I knew momma would say no. So, as soon as momma parked the car and got busy with her household chores, I dropped my book satchel at the back door, took off my half slip, draped it over a rose bush in the flower bed and headed for Little Polly's. I played for a while before I was found. It was one of my first remembrances of knowing I'd get a spanking from my momma if I did something she'd warned me not to do, but I did it anyway.

It continued as I got older. She pulled me aside at my thirteenth birthday party, which she was hosting, to tell me, "You need to tone it down. You are acting a little too full of yourself and people don't like that. You won't have any friends left. Don't talk so loud. Don't forget to say thank you when the girls leave." As I entered adolescence, the list of her rules lengthened as did her vigilance in making sure I obeyed them. Like Demeter desiring to ensure Persephone's innocence, my mother was bent on protecting me from the world that she experienced as dangerous for young girls. She would armor me with her regulations.

Mother knew the cultural expectations of girl children. If they were instinctive, wild, curious, creative – they needed to be tamed, she thought. She tried over and over to tame me. I don't know when she discovered that her own untamed emotions and physical vulnerabilities were a way to rein me in, but she attempted to convince me that she needed me to care for her. From my earliest years, I was caught between my need to care for her and my need to escape from her.

My mother and I have spent a lifetime taking turns caring for one another. My polio was followed by her hysterectomy. Her hysterectomy was followed by my tuberculosis. My tuberculosis was followed by her pneumonia. Her pneumonia was followed by my nephritis. My nephritis was followed by her "nervous condition." Her "nervous condition" issued in my good health. My good health made it so much easier to pay attention to her needs.

When I was thirteen, I belonged to my church's Girls Auxiliary. We were having a mother/daughter tea and I wanted momma to attend. She dressed up, walked in with me, and then headed straight to a table to seat herself. She asked me to get her a cup of punch and some cookies and bring them to her. I understood why. It was a pattern we had engaged in since I was old enough to understand that her hands shook with a palsy that was delivered with her at birth. She feared carrying her own punch and cookies because she might spill them and be embarrassed. I took care of her by bringing the refreshments to her. I learned early on to stifle the thoughts I was having, the thoughts that creeped into my mind and made their way into my journals, only to be marked through later, lest they be discovered when she snooped in my things – *I want a momma like Barbara's or Carolyn's or Lydia's – a momma who takes care of herself*. Guilt inevitably followed those thoughts.

The Demeter/Persephone story teaches us that separating from the mother is a particularly challenging process for a daughter because she has to separate from the one who is the same as herself. This may produce a conflict between wanting the mother's love and approval and wanting a different life than the mother's. The mother archetype's opposite expressions - sustenance and protection versus suffocation and death - present a girl with the choice to embrace the mother or rebel against the mother.

* * *

I have been struggling with this paradox my entire life. I recall being in a writing workshop. The instructor had just told us to write from our obsession. I had a trunkload of material ready. Still I keep waiting for a new obsession – one to come in and take the place of the one I have with my mother. I am obsessed with both mothering and being mothered.

Obsession – what does it mean? Haunted, besieged, dominating the mind – these are the synonyms of obsession.

And what is the root of this obsession of mine? I have been writing about my mother my entire life – in my diaries, journals, and writing workshops. She is the stuff of my dreams. I sighed with recognition when I read in Helen Luke's, *Such Stuff as Dreams Are Made On* – "*Some of the paradoxes of my nature in my childhood and youth – indeed all through life –spring surely from this double nature of my mother's love and its overwhelming all-pervasive importance to me. On the one hand was the integrity and truth of her conscious love, on the other her unconscious projection of her emotional life onto me.*"

In Jungian terms, my obsession with my mother has a name, The Mother Complex. It has both positive and negative characteristics. Positively, Demeter love is homecoming, shelter, silence, giving of life. Negatively, it is the averted face, letting life pass by like a dream, refusing to see reality. I have spent a life-time ignoring the reality of my mother's hurtful actions or making excuses for them. Who was I protecting – her or me? Her legacy to me was a life of uncertainty. Which mother would show up today - the nurturing, protective, cheerleading mother or the raging, punishing, abandoning mother? If I wasn't prepared, I'd be ambushed, an easy target.

Like the time she'd made herself a new yellow linen dress to wear to see me perform in a high school play in which I was cast It appeared she was over her anger that I'd tried out for the play and would not talk me out of doing it. I was excited to have auditioned and won the part, and I was thrilled that, after weeks of rehearsal, tonight was opening night. I arrived home from school to find her locked in her room. Bobby reported that Momma said she wasn't going to my play. When Daddy got home, I told him. He knocked on the door, saying, "Charlyne, open up now. We have to leave for Beverly Ann's play in a little while."

"I'm not going. I don't want her to be an actress. I'm not supporting that hogwash."

"Let's talk. Let me in," Daddy begged.

"I don't care if she goes or not," I lied.

"You don't mean that," Daddy said.

"Yes, I do," I lied again.

"Beverly Ann," he said.

"She just wants to ruin this for me," I cried.

"No, your mother loves you," Daddy insisted.

"This doesn't look like love to me," I said.

I don't know how he convinced her to go, or how I ever had the wherewithal to show up, much less remember my lines, but I did.

* * *

In childhood, I had a recurring dream. A wolf wearing coveralls was chasing me around our house on the hill, the one my parents built. We were running in my mother's flowerbeds beside the house, and they were filled with blooming hollyhocks. Out of breath and weary, I ran and ran and ran, always just barely ahead of the wolf. The myth of an individual life, Jung said, is often foreshadowed in the dreams of childhood.

The dream first occurred after my mother "left me." She and Daddy had a fight. She scooped Bobby up in her arms, ran to the car, and drove away. It was nighttime, and I was terrified.

"Where is Momma going?" I asked Daddy.

"For a ride. She'll be back soon," he replied.

Daddy said The Lord's Prayer with me, and tucked me in. When I fell asleep in my new maple bed in my pink and turquoise room, she was still gone.

The next morning Daddy and I were having milk toast for breakfast when Momma walked in carrying Bobby in one arm and a sack from the bakery in her other hand. She was cheery, announcing she'd spent the night at Grandma's, as if nothing had happened. I was skeptical. Who is this woman I'd wondered. Last night she left crying. This morning she is happy, offering me sweets.

"I've got to go to work," Daddy said.

"I want to go with you," I told him.

"Don't be ridiculous," Momma admonished. "You can't go to work with your daddy. You have to stay here with Bobby and me."

I didn't want to stay there with her. What if she leaves me again? I thought. What if Daddy leaves? I felt I was her hostage. I escaped to the outdoors and the world I created in play.

\* \* \*

Sitting on the sofa here in my study at 2:30 in the morning, I am still waiting for my mother to explain to me how she could have abandoned me – her daughter. It is as unlikely that she will explain it now as it was sixty years ago. Years later, I was still mourning my mother's departure, by becoming a father's daughter, trying to control what happened instead of just allowing it to happen. And even now, I am still escaping to the outdoors and the worlds of work and play that I create. At least now, though, I sometimes recognize that is what I am doing – sometimes, not always.

\* \* \*

Growing up, our house was often so full of emotion that the walls seemed expanded, pulsating. It was emotion that ranged from full blown joy to demonic rage. By that time I had become accustomed to the uncertainty, the not knowing which mother would show up at a given moment.

I loved the momma who took us dewberry picking in the summer, who let us roam the creeks and branches while she and her friends gathered mustang grapes to use for jelly, juice, and popsicles, and who drove to truck farms, picked corn, beans, peas, tomatoes, cantaloupes, and watermelons while we played hide-and-seek in between the corn rows. Momma prided herself on her canning and freezing skills. She was an excellent cook. Like Demeter, she showed her generosity through sharing this food with others. Friends and family were welcome at our table *anytime*.

In fact, when one of Daddy's cousins needed a place to stay while he worked in a town near us, Momma said, "Sure, he's welcome here." Another time, one of Daddy's cousins was "drying out," and he stayed at our house until he could "get back on his feet." Our cousins sometimes spent weeks with us during the summer or Christmas break.

But then, there was the momma who frightened me. Daddy dodged when she threw cups or vases, anything within her reach. When he left for awhile to escape her fury, she cried as she cleaned up the mess. Bobby ran from this momma when she threatened a spanking. This momma said no unpredictably, depending on the mood she was in. Daddy once brought me a pair of white cowboy boots with green decorative stitching. It was June, time for the Junior Championship High School Rodeo. Those boots were perfect. I pranced and preened in front of the mirror, focused on my feet in those elegant boots. "Eddie," she shrieked, "who's going to take care of those boots? They are totally impractical for a child. Take them back. Get brown ones." He did. Why didn't he tell her no? Why did she get her way? I will tell her no, I thought. I am like a wild horse. She will have to break me. I will not go unheard in this house. I will speak out. Little did I know that speaking and being heard were two different things.

Early in the morning while still wondering if I will rush to my mother's side, my mind wanders to the time when my son was twelve and we were on a family ski vacation. He wanted expensive moon boots.

I was surprised when his dad said yes because he was always complaining to me about the amount of money we spent. I argued that Jeff didn't need the boots, would use them for a short time, and that it was too much money to spend. He got the boots. Sitting in the dark, I wonder if my son remembers that.

* * *

Jung says the mother has three essential aspects – goodness, passion, and darkness. I think of my own mother stories and what aspects they demonstrate. Who is the mother out in the light? Who is the mother hiding in the shadow?

* * *

I look at the clock. It is three a.m. , and I am still uncertain about whether to stay or go. What is wrong with me? She is asleep. I will go in the morning. *But,* what if my mother can't sleep? What if she is frightened after the fall, the hospital visit, and the stitches? What if they've restrained her and she is trying to get out of the bed? It is hard for my mother to accept boundaries and restraints, hard for me to accept that she must do so.

* * *

I think of times when my mother forgot where she ended and I began.

When I returned from my two-day honeymoon during the Thanksgiving holiday with a desire to study for my finals and prepare for the student teaching I was to begin in January, I was unable to. I had accepted my new mother-in-law's offer to take our wedding gifts from the tables set up in my parents' living room to our duplex before we returned home. To my surprise, when we walked in late on Sunday night, there were no presents. There was a note from my mother-in-law telling me that my mother refused to let her move the gifts. "It's my job to do that. She should have asked me," the note quoted my mother.

It wasn't long before the phone rang and she was raging at me. "*What* possessed you to invite *that* woman into *my* home to remove *your* gifts? You are so ungrateful! I made your brides' dress, your attendants' dresses, paid for the caterer, and you treat me like this!"

I hung up.

In minutes, my daddy was knocking on our front door. He looked like he needed sleep. His green eyes had lost their usual sparkle. He wore his standard Sunday clothing, navy slacks and a starched long sleeved white shirt. The tie was gone and the top button was unbuttoned. I wondered if he'd gone to church this morning. I hugged him and let him in. He said, "Your momma is devastated. She thinks you don't love and appreciate her. You need to come to the house and tell her you're sorry."

"Sorry for what?" I asked. "She should be sorry. Now I have to move all those things myself. I knew she couldn't do it because she has the childcare business all day every day. I'm at school and work, so I accepted someone else's offer to do it and now she created a problem for us both."

"Think about this," my father pleaded. "Remember everything your momma did to make this nice wedding for you. She loves you so much."

"I'll think about it, but I'm not going there now. I'm tired."

It was days before my mother and I spoke. The gifts remained at her house. I don't even remember how they finally got to mine.

Nine years later, my husband took his share of those same gifts from our home on a Saturday while the children and I were gone. My neighbor told me a woman helped him move out. I called my mother to ask if I could bring my children, ages seven, three, and two, to stay with her for a few days. I needed to find my husband, the father of my children, and see what the future held for us. I found him at work on Monday. He wanted a divorce. I went to pick up my children and bring them home. I arrived at Mother's, told her we were getting a divorce, and shared my situation, saying I planned on staying in San Antonio where I had a job, friends, and a church home.

"That's insane. You can't stay there, alone with three kids. You need to move here, and I'll take care of the kids while you work." "I already have a job I like, childcare I trust, a church, and friends there. I'm not moving here."

I had the two-year-old in my arms and the seven-and three-year olds at my side. My mother pulled back her hand and slapped me hard on the cheek. Tears stung my eyes and rolled down my cheeks.

"Run to the car," I said to my children. I did the same.

My mother did not speak to me for some time. Demeter can experience a child's growing autonomy as an emotional loss for herself. She feels rejected, useless, and can become hostile or depressed, even actively vindictive.

Demeter underwent a transformation when her daughter, Persephone, was abducted by Hades. She was grief-stricken and devastated by the loss, but she did not sit back and do nothing. She took action. Demeter made a deal with Hades. She would have Persephone six months and Hades would have her for six months.

Women wrenched from the mother by patriarchy itself or the patriarchal marriage partner have usually grown up with long lists of shoulds and oughts – the rules and regulations. They often become father's daughters, at ease in the world of the masculine, enemies of the very mother whose love they so desire, alienated from the goddess spirit that has been exiled from our world for thousands of years. Like Persephone, they must descend into the underworld and reacquaint themselves with the power and passion of the feminine, and then return to the waiting arms of the mother, their own Demeter. Some women have had such negative mother experiences that they don't believe their mother will be waiting for them upon their return from the dark.

My mother left me alone for awhile. Alone, with the failure of my marriage, the responsibility of single parenthood, a child's birth defect, the potential for new love. I was in and out of the dark a lot.

After this time of separation, Mother called to say, "I bet you could use a rest from the kids. I'd love to have them come for the weekend. Meet me at our half-way point – the Holiday Inn parking lot in New Braunfels."

I did.

Other separations and reunitings have taken place during the years. When I moved to Colorado from Texas, I was scolded, "you are taking my grandchildren away from me." Though I purchased her an airline ticket each summer and each Christmas, she said the visits were too short and mourned the loss of proximity to her grandchildren.

I had my own Demeter/Persephone experience when my two

teenaged daughters left Colorado and spent eight months living with my mother in Texas. The mixture of loss and relief mingled as I entered my own desert and struggled with my own demons. To my surprise, my mother never chided me. She held the space, as mothers do, for something new to be born. Hollow objects – vessels and ovens – are symbols of this capacity. Spiritually, the mother is represented in symbols that show our longing for redemption – paradise, the kingdom of God, the church, heaven, earth, woods, seas, the underworld, the moon.

* * *

The night is almost over. I did not go to my mother at one or two or three a.m. I have been with my mother all night, however. It is almost four, and I decide to sleep for a few hours and then go to see her, when it is light.

I know she will be waiting there for me.

# CHAPTER SIX

## DANCING WITH DEATH

## PERSEPHONE

## GODDESS OF DEATH, RENEWAL, AND TRANSFORMATION

*"every now and then I have a quiet chat with the skeletons in my closet – just so they don't come looking for me on their own."*
- erin smith, from a purchased greeting card

Year Three

# Dancing with Death

I doze fitfully and awaken at 5:30 a.m. with a case of the blues. I know I need to sleep a little more, but I decide to get ready and go to the nursing home to check on my mother. Larry was up at his usual five a.m. so I can smell the coffee brewing and I go to the kitchen to get a cup. I choose my mug from the many collected on our travels or given to us as gifts. A *Gone With the Wind* mug, given to my by my youngest daughter is right in front of me. I fill it with French roast and think of how much my parents had in common with Scarlett O'Hara and Rhett Butler. Rhett desired to be what Scarlett wanted and needed, but Scarlett had her own path to follow. Now I am moving slowly on my own path, weighed down by sorrow. My mother is not only losing her mind, she is losing her ability to get around in the world, to walk. I want to shake the blues, but I just can't.

\* \* \*

Mother had often warned me not to bring the blues into her house. Her typical response to my wanting to share my feelings of loss or sadness with her was, "I don't want you to be blue. Let's talk about something happy and get your mind off all that."

I just wanted to be heard. I didn't need to dwell on it, but I wanted acknowledgement from someone I loved and who loved me that I *was* heard, that it was a tough time, and that it was okay to feel the feelings that go with hard times – sadness, anger, powerlessness. Mother couldn't do that for me. After trying to get her to, to no avail, I'd feel worse than I did before because I was obviously insensitive to my mother's need for me to be happy. Now, crying for my mother in her dementia, I was reminded of the years I'd spent in therapy trying to understand why it was so hard for me to express my feelings. My mother's feelings took up all the space in the house. There wasn't room for anyone else's. If I complained to my daddy, he'd say, "You're strong. She's sick. Don't feel that way. You don't want your feelings to take control of you."

I think of something my daughter, Whitney, said to me years

ago. "Mom, one of the things I'm having to work through is that you always wanted me to feel good. You didn't want me to be sad or angry or unhappy. I remember when I'd come to you with one of those 'bad' feelings, you'd pull me into your lap, stroke my hair, and say, 'You're so beautiful, you're so smart, you can get over this. Let's think of something to do to get your mind off it.'"

My discovery that I come from a long line of women who are "bluesphobic" has been an *ah ha*. In questioning my mother years ago about this inherited phobia, she affirmed, "My momma and her momma didn't like anyone bringing the blues into their house either. They thought it was a good idea to do something to take your mind off it."

A phobia is a persistent and obsessive fear or aversion to something. Why are the women on my maternal side of the family so fearful of the blues? Recognizing this fear of the blues as a phobia, I had to ask myself why did they avoid doing battle with the blues by thinking happy thoughts, doing something, often for others, or working harder and harder? That all may be good in theory, but.....a blue feeling is a hard thing to ignore. It will keep popping up at the most inopportune time, nudging and poking and wanting attention.

A friend of mine says an emotion is an unacknowledged feeling. My mother is *full* of emotion – feelings of which she is unaware. That emotion has always spilled out all over me. I long to experience my feelings. What I imagine my blues desires is the attention of someone like Aretha Franklin or Patti LaBelle. My blues yearns to get pulled down into my gut and sung out from that deep place with all the wailing and moaning, and ultimately rejoicing, that can be mustered. My blues wants to be welcomed into my house. Can I do it? Can I sit with my mother's fall, make peace with my own darkness before I rush to her side?

\* \* \*

Persephone represents the darkness into which we must descend in order to be reborn. Persephone must be torn from her role as her mother's daughter so that she can enter the depths of her own soul. Years ago I read Doris Lessing's *Golden Notebook* and the line that remains with me to this day is *"a breakdown can be a breakthrough."* My mother's periodic breakdowns provided windows into my own soul.

Mother's descents into darkness cast a shadow over our world just as Persephone's disappearance into the bowels of the earth to join Hades caused the flowers to cease blooming and the trees to shed their leaves under a fallow or barren moon.

Dressing to leave for my trip to the nursing home, darkness descends on me again as I ponder my mother's fall last night, her treatment, and her being alone with strangers in an emergency room.

* *

It is early morning. Driving this two-lane Texas highway I am enveloped in darkness. In this hour before dawn there is only the glow of my headlights before me. The road stretches out in front of me with its curves and straight places. Though I travel this road often and am familiar with it, I find myself alert to the possibility of the unfamiliar hidden in the dark ahead. A pack of dogs is suddenly revealed in my headlights, and I brake to avoid hitting it. The car skids as I hit a puddle of water left by last night's rain, a reminder that no road is the same road twice. Dawn is peeking through the charcoal sky, a hint of fleshy pink To the east the pink turns to coral, the color and shape of flamingo feathers. The trees are black shadows silhouetted against the pink and blue and gray. As the light grows stronger, the shadow trees disappear, revealing in their place the leafy green of summer trees. The sun commands the sky and reflects off the water of a pond, blinding me with its brightness. I wonder to myself how we are like the highway, the sky, the trees, the water. What is revealed of us as we move from darkness into light?

I reach for my travel coffee cup to take a sip. I turn it up too much and coffee splashes out onto my white shirt. I reach for a container of wet ones on the passenger seat and turn the steering wheel as I reach. I am too slow to correct and am already on the narrow shoulder of the road about to spin into the grassy ditch. I slow to a stop. I am discomfited. I decide to sit for a minute, clean the coffee stains from my shirt with a Wet One, and catch my breath. Then I remember. This is the same highway on which my mother attempted to kill herself in front of my daddy, Bobby, and me when I was thirteen. The thought of it makes me begin to weep. How many times have I driven on this same road and not thought of that day? Maybe never. Why am I thinking of this now? Is it because she is dying slowly in front of me these days? How do I bear witness to my mother's death? I pull over to the road's shoulder. My tears are blinding me.

\* \* \*

At 50 mph on a two lane highway on a busy Sunday afternoon, Daddy grabs for Momma's arm with one hand while holding the steering wheel with the other. He struggles in traffic to keep the car on the road as she screams, "I want to die!" and tries to jump out of the car.

"Charlyne, you'll kill us all," Daddy shouts, as the car swerves onto the gravelly shoulder of the road.

"Mommy, Mommy, please don't jump. Pleeease...." Bobby begs.

I sit in silence.

Momma has tumbled out of the car onto the gravel. She has struggled out of Daddy's grip and is rolling onto the grass. The car stops. Is she hurt? Dead?

"I'm scared," Bobby says. "Are you scared?"

"I hate her," I reply. To myself, I think, who is this woman? I'm afraid of her. I can't wait to leave home.

It was only weeks ago that she was sobbing and screaming at Daddy in the kitchen. I was in my room engrossed in *Gone With the Wind* when she called for Bobby and me to come. I didn't want to go. She called again. I went.

I can still see her standing there. Her nose was running and her hair was mussed. Daddy, head in his hands, was in his chair at the kitchen table, saying, "Don't do this, Charlyne. Don't do this. You'll regret it. I know you'll regret it."

She couldn't be stopped. She was like a runaway train on a path to destroy everything in its way. Screaming and crying, she yelled out, "Beverly Ann and Bobby, do you know what your daddy has to hold over my head. Do you know?"

Bobby and I stand in the kitchen, not sure where this is taking us and not wanting to find out. I turn to leave the room. She grabs me by the arm and says, "You are going to hear this. I won't have your daddy hold this over my head any longer!"

I can't breathe. The smell of supper lingers in the air, something fried. The table has been cleared and all the dirty dishes are stacked on the counter by the sink full of soapy water. The gas range is covered with pots and pans waiting for their turn in the dishwater. I look down at the linoleum floor on which I stand.

"I was married before. I was very young. He left me. I had an abortion. Your grandma, my mother, flushed my gold wedding band down the commode when the divorce was final. Are you happy, Eddie? Are you happy now?"

She grabs the car keys off the table and leaves the house.

The air is hot. The room is silent. I look at Bobby and Daddy. No one says anything. I go to my room. I get my dictionary out and look up abortion. It says miscarriage. I look up miscarriage. It says aborted pregnancy. I wonder if my mother miscarried naturally or aborted intentionally.

On a road trip with my mother once, several years ago, I said, "Tell me about your first marriage."

I was driving. Mother was in the passenger seat. She looked straight ahead and replied, "Never mention that to me again."

When I returned home, I called my cousin, Molly, who worked in the courthouse and asked her to look for my mother's divorce papers.

"I didn't know Aunt Charlyne had been married before," she gasped. "When did you find out?"

"It's a long story," I reply. "I'll share it with you some time. Do you think you can find the divorce papers or a marriage license."

"I'll sure try."

She mailed me a copy of the papers. Emboldened by my proof, I requested Molly ask her momma and daddy to tell her what they knew about the marriage and its dissolution. She called to report that they had two different stories. Her daddy, my mother's brother, said, "I drove Sister to a nearby town to marry the man. Our parents didn't approve of the marriage and wouldn't attend." Molly's momma said, "Your grandma threw a fit, calling Charlyne names and threatening to disown her. Charlyne defied her, married him anyway, and then came home when he left her for another woman. Your grandma wanted it annulled, but Charlyne said annulling it was saying it never happened, and it did. She got a divorce and a job in Houston."

\* \* \*

I sit in the car on the side of the road and observe the mess I've made. I don't know how many Wet Ones I've used to reduce the coffee stains on my blouse to mere hints of beige. The passenger seat is covered with discarded wipes. My CD's slid off the seat and onto the floor when I left the highway. I hear Leonard Cohen still singing in the background. How long have I been sitting here thinking about my mother's attempt to kill herself and wondering if it was because of that secret she carried around. To this day I don't know if my mother miscarried naturally or aborted intentionally. Now there is no one to ask. *And,* I still want to know. Why do I need to know? Why is my mother's story so important to me? Is it because she kept something such a secret, so hidden, so undiscussable. Does every woman have a hidden story, a story they do not what to share? I love the Muriel Rukeyser quotation – *"What would happen if one woman told the truth about her life? The world would split open."* Adrienne Rich says, *"The loss of the daughter to the mother, the mother to the daughter, is the essential female tragedy."*

I am losing my mother before I've even gotten to really know her or appreciate her. I think that, but is it really true? These last three years of being with her as dementia moves in are revealing to me the essence of my mother. Can I be there to bear witness to the light *and* the dark?

I have a long history of resisting the darkness. I want to turn my head from images that take me from the light – the tattered homeless man urinating in the Denver parking lot, the stretchers carrying bloody victims from the most recent Baghdad marketplace bombing, the mud slides in California, even my own child being stuck and poked for countless surgical procedures.

In 1989, my husband, Larry and I attended a Community Building Retreat with Scott Peck. Having read *The Road Less Traveled, People of the Lie,* and *The Different Drum,* I had anticipated that I would be thrilled to be sitting in this circle in Knoxville, Tennessee with my "guru" facilitating. By noon of the first day I wanted to leave. I had sat in a circle of sixty-five people in a standard hotel conference room from 8:30 - Noon. We still did not know each other's names, hometowns, or reason for being here. As the author of a team building program, *Creating Community in Organizations,* I had been facilitating groups ranging in size from ten to four hundred for years, and I was frustrated by what I considered poor facilitation on Dr. Peck's part. Hotel staff had come and gone throughout the morning, refilling large silver coffee urns, restocking soft drinks in tubs of crushed ice, and refilling fruit and bread trays.

At the close of the morning session, Larry and I went back to our hotel room where Larry proceeded to "talk me down."

"I didn't come here to listen to people relive their childhood abuses and traumas hour on end. That circle has sixty-five people in it. How many more stories will we have to hear?" I asked.

"We've only been here for one morning. We have three more days. Give it a while. You know how upset you'd be if someone left your workshop at the beginning and didn't give it a chance," Larry said.

I returned to the circle.

By mid-afternoon, I spoke aloud to the group my concern saying something to the effect of, "People need to move past their childhoods and get on with life. Are we going to spend the entire weekend talking about people's problems?"

Jerry, a smiling, perfectly groomed man who reminded me of several preachers in my growing up years was sitting near me. He looked directly at me and said, "Beverly, these stories have shaped us. These stories *are* our lives. I used to feel like you do. Now I don't. I feel sorry for you."

His saying he felt sorry for me only made me angrier. *But* **I** stayed in that circle from Thursday through Sunday trying to manage my discomfort by talking with Larry, journaling, drinking wine, and walking.

It would be a year before I began to get it, why Jerry *should* have felt sorry for me. By now, I felt sorry for myself. Stephen Levine, a Buddhist writer, says we must have mercy on ourselves before we can have mercy on others. For me that meant looking at my own life, telling my own story, being with what is *and* was.

I still find myself wanting to look away, but I can't do it as easily anymore. Now I sit affixed to my spot through shootings, kidnappings, bombings, natural catastrophes. I am being called to bear witness, to behold the world in its wholeness – light and dark. I remember the little girl I once was – the one who hid her scary comic books so she wouldn't be reminded of what frightened her. I recall a Christmas shopping trip to Houston when I was eight and how I would turn my eyes from the amputee on the corner in rags selling pencils or the drooling mentally retarded woman with the tin cup extended hand. At ten I sang in a children's choir that visited the local nursing home. I purposely stood in the back row to avoid the gnarled hands reaching out to touch us.

\* \* \*

Mother must have wanted it to go away too. Doctors through the years gave her the prescriptions for "mother's little helpers," Valium, Xanax, Ativan. Recently, one of the aides at the nursing home told me in a moment of confidence that a number of the women in the secured unit were like my mom, needing their helpers. Now I hear them cry and call out when I am visiting. The men often pace. I have recently started sitting with one or another of the residents when my mother is asleep in her chair. Sometimes I help feed someone who can't feed herself. I know the name of each of the residents in my mother's unit. I comfort them when they call for their momma or sister or brother. I sit amid drooling, kicking, raging, whimpering, yelling, and I worship. This is a difficult and sacred space I have been invited into.

Here I am in the 21st century, recently turned sixty, and only now have I developed the courage to really look, to behold all this world offers – the joy and the pain, the beauty and the ugliness, the exultation and the degradation, the generosity and the greed. Looking reminds me that sometimes I am impotent and powerless, and sometimes moved by compassion to action. The choice *is* mine.

\* \* \*

The gift of having a mother who danced with death fueled my desire for solitude, silence, and introspection. Like Persephone, my mother could be abducted by a reality she saw as cruel, inequitable, and wrong. She could sink into the darkness of despair or vibrate with anxiety, sometimes calling for death. When this occurred periodically, I sought solace in my room with my journal and pen or a book or outdoors alone exploring creek beds and woods. I was bereft. The Aphrodite/Hestia/Athena mother I knew had vanished and I was frightened by this mother who shrieked, threatened, longed to die, or disappeared.

I've had a lifetime of practice going from the light to the dark and back again. My journals have these explorations recorded. I began keeping a diary at age eight, changing the name to journal at age sixteen. Diary or journal, whatever I named them, these books house the accumulation of a lifetime of reflections.

These journals are filled with promises to myself never to be like her.

But then, my mother's dementia came on the heels of my husband's early retirement, my son's divorce, the birth of my oldest daughter's second child, my youngest daughter's marriage, our move from a city of over a million to a village of thirty-three hundred, and my consulting business faltering as a result of the move. Depression came to visit me. It didn't appear as I imagined depression would, clothed in black, putting me to bed for months. It adapted to my location. Depression wore a swimsuit and rode on the back of my bicycle to the beach, weighing me down, taking away my speed. I stood in front of the shelves at the local grocery store and looked at the hundreds of detergent choices. I couldn't choose. I had always been decisive and now I was rendered opinionless. The phone would ring and I would ignore it. I got mad at the friends who had known me longest. I wanted them to know what was going on in my mind even if I couldn't express it verbally. If they didn't know, I didn't want to have to tell them. Depression argued with me when I wanted to do what I'd always done, making me explain why. Often I had no explanation. When I argued too long and too hard, it invited in its colleague, illness, in the form of my first case of shingles. I was stopped whether I liked it or not.

The shingles whipped me, put me to bed in my peaceful palmetto green bedroom, rendered me motionless. I lay there in that room looking at a photograph on my natural wicker bedstand of Larry and me climbing Dunn River Falls in Ocho Rios, Jamaica. I tried to remember the woman in that picture, me, happily laughing out loud. I couldn't. I had a stack of books by Caroline Myss, books on the body and healing, in bed with me. Surely, I could find an answer on these pages. The medication for shingles gave me a urinary tract infection. I looked up shingles in Louise Hay's *Heal Your Life*. It said, "waiting for the other shoe to drop." I looked up urinary tract infection and it said, "being pissed off at someone." Louise sure nailed me. As I lay there in my bed, lamenting, "what now," I went through my list of all the things that had hurt in my life, all the losses, and then simmered in my own anger over it.

I read in an AARP Bulletin that over nineteen million Americans experience persistent, or clinical depression. Of these nineteen million, six million are over age sixty-five. Going to Thomas Moore's *Original Self*, I read, "*Depression wears many faces....To enter depression creatively, it might be best to start by describing the feeling in the most ordinary and concrete terms. Simple, descriptive words would convey the experience....For all its pain and dangers, depression can be humanizing, provided that we imagine it humanly....We carry the depression of life in our hearts, thinking that the weight must be personal, unaware that it is the world around us that is suffering.*"

It was time for me to stop ignoring my feelings about all of these things in my life. Jean Shinoda Bolen says, in *Goddesses in Older Women*, "*Persephone will stay the eternal maiden or the eternal victim, until she stops withholding herself, denying the truth about her situation, and learns from her experience. Her route is circuitous rather than a straight line; she has dabbled and gathered experiences. Significant and strong personalities told her who she was and what should make her happy....*" I had had a lifetime of someone telling me what to feel and what not to feel. The author, Henry Ward Beecher wrote, "*What the mother sings to the cradle goes all the way down to the coffin.*" Now, I am determined to listen to my mother's song, no matter how painful.

\* \* \*

In the nursing home parking lot, the mirror on the visor reveals my puffy eyes and tear stained cheeks. I have cried all the way here. I blow my nose, wipe my tears, search for my compact and lipstick. I can't go in looking like I've been sobbing. I powder my nose, put on my lipstick, and prepare to see my mother.

As soon as I enter the secured unit, I spot her sitting in a wheelchair by the window in the unit's living room. Tiffany, a nurses' aide, who is always cheerful and happy, approaches me. She has on mint green scrubs sprinkled with teddy bears.

"Your mom took quite a tumble last night. I wasn't here, but Melody told me about it when we changed shifts."

"How is she doing this morning?" I ask.

"She ate her breakfast. She's not saying much, and she seems more confused than usual."

"Thanks. I'll talk to you later."

"Mother," I say, and I draw up a chair, sit down, and take her hand in mine.

Her face is bruised and swollen. She has a line of stitches on her forehead above her left eye, and is wearing a nightgown that doesn't belong to her – one more indignity to suffer.

She tears up as she looks at me. "Where have you been?" she says. "I fell last night and now they won't let me walk."

"I'm so sorry," I reply. I kiss her cheek and squeeze her hand.

"Momma," she addresses me. "Momma, don't let them make me sit in this wheelchair. I want to get up and walk."

That is all the encouragement I need. I say, "Mother, I'm going to see the Administrator, Ross. I'll tell him you want to use your walker and you should be allowed to do that."

Ever vigilant, I have been looking around to see what could have caused her to stumble. Believe it or not, they are painting the area and there are paint cans, drop cloths, and ladders in the hall. My thought - what is wrong with this place? They should be more careful of the residents' safety. Now I am not just concerned for my mother, but I am standing up for all the residents.

Because I cannot sit with the pain of my mother's increasing losses, I spring into action. Instead of being with her, holding her hand, seeing her body ravaged by the fall, a symbol of her lost mobility, I go to see the nursing home administrator with my litany of complaints. When his response is unsatisfactory, I call the State's ombudsman line to report the incident. I take photographs of the littered hallway. Sure, the complaints are legitimate. There *are* obstacles in the walkways of this secured unit. However, I don't see the obstacles in my own mind and heart. It is too hard for me to admit my mother is leaving me and feel the grief and sorrow of that loss.

\* \* \*

I go out and sit in my car in the nursing home parking lot. I can't stop the tears. My mother has left me so many times in my life. When did I start leaving her?

I can think of three times when my mother locked herself in a windowless bathroom and turned on the gas in the space heater. Twice I was a teenager. I watched as Daddy banged on the door and Bobby and I stood by in alarm, sniffing the fumes, and fearing for her life. The drama would end with Daddy hitting the door with his shoulder and opening it by sheer force. She would be lying on the floor sobbing, hysterical. Daddy would go to her, pull her to himself, and say to us, "Your momma just doesn't mean to do this. She's sick. She needs help. She loves you. Go on outside, ride your bikes, try to forget about it. Everything's going to be okay."

The third time she did it, I was twenty-three with a husband, a one-year-old child of my own, and a full-time teaching job. My husband and I lived in a historic home we had just purchased and were restoring located two miles from my parents' residence. Because we were a one car family, I'd asked my husband to drop me off there for supper while he attended a rehearsal for a musical he was accompanying. After supper, Mother and I had argued about something, a topic I do not remember to this day. It was probably one of the many arguments we had as I asserted myself, making my own decisions, resisting her control. Instead of waiting for my husband to pick me up as planned, which would have necessitated my listening to her criticisms and commands, I loaded my son's diaper bag, positioned him on one hip, and left her house.

I walked the two miles home.

Sometime later, Daddy called. "Your mother is locked in the bathroom with the gas on. Please come."

"Daddy, call Dr. Reading," I replied. "Mother needs help, professional help. I can't give her the help she needs. It's never going to be okay unless she gets help. She's been going to Dr. Reading for years. He knows her. *And* us."

I hung up. Terrified, I waited across town in my kitchen. Guilt ridden, I wondered what kind of daughter doesn't go to the aid of her mother.

It seemed like an eternity before Daddy called and said, "Dr. Reading wants to talk to you."

"Okay," I answered.

When I heard Dr. Reading's voice, I pictured him with his serious face, black rimmed glasses, pen in the pocket of his short sleeved shirt, a man who wasted no words and pulled no punches. "Beverly," he said, "your dad asked me to talk to you. I want to admit your mother to St.

Mark's in Austin. They have an excellent psychiatric ward. She needs to rest, *and* she needs to talk to someone about the things that are bothering her. They have a psychiatrist that I've referred several patients to. Any questions?"

"How long will she be there?" I asked.

"For as long as it takes," he replied. "Then she'll need some out-patient care, and that will mean some trips back and forth to Austin. We don't have a psychiatrist here in town. Maybe you can drive her sometimes."

"Maybe," I said in a way that belied my relief at hearing his calm words telling me that he recognized she needed help and was getting it for her.

"I've ordered an ambulance, and they will be here to pick her up soon. She won't be able to have any visitors for at least a week or so."

I breathed with relief when he said that. I was not ready to see her.

That was her last suicide attempt. Her future cries for help shifted to her physical needs and ailments and my brother's and my neglect of her.

\* \* \*

Here I am, out in the car in front of my mother's nursing home after my visit, attempting to process the experience of her fall and my response to it.

\* \* \*

In Persephone's story, she must eat the pomegranate seeds before leaving the underworld so that she can return, but not as a victim. She does not want to be identified with her mother when she returns. Eating the seeds represented her ability to integrate and digest her experiences and to give birth to her own new personality. Once the experience is taken in, Persephone is able to emerge as a woman, no longer an innocent maiden or a mother's daughter. Now she has realized she has responsibilities and choices *and* the self-confidence earned through her experiences in the underworld. Using those experiences, Persephone makes use of her empathy, imagination, and her relationship to the collective unconscious.

Persephone beckons when there has been a loss. In *The Goddess Within*, the Wooglers, Jennifer and Roger, describe loss as a *"wrenching away of energy from the image of some loved person, place, or way of life into some huge, empty emotional void."* They continue by saying, *"a part of us always accompanies the lost person or beloved attachment into the underworld. And when this happens, that part of us is not fully available for normal life, and we need to honor this process, not seek to falsely cheer ourselves up."* Persephone is the daughter who has lost her mother.

\* \* \*

I can no longer deny that my mother is lost to me. Sitting in my car alone in a parking lot, I am grieving my mother's increasing dementia, and, at this moment, her latest physical fall, but most importantly, a lifetime of losing my mother. I sit and grieve the loss of an all-powerful father and a longed-for mother who could give me a perfect childhood.

\* \* \*

Years ago, 1993 to be exact, in a period of six months, my husband had a stroke, my son eloped, my oldest daughter graduated from college, and my youngest daughter moved into an apartment of her own. One morning during that time, I awoke from a dream of Latin soldiers marching in perfect formation, meticulously groomed. There was one glaring problem, they had large knives stuck in their foreheads, right between the brow, the third eye. Blood was trickling down their faces from their wounds. They looked straight ahead, through me, as I screamed for their assistance. I was being pursued by bandits in a South American jungle. I had witnessed their attack on a man at a golf course. The soldiers marched straight toward the golf course.

The truth was, I had never been in a South American jungle. On my one trip to work in South America, I stayed in the heart of that Argentine city, Buenos Aires. I saw no knives and few soldiers.

I was haunted for days by these images and worked with the dream as I'd learned to do from a book and in a workshop. I chose three symbols from that dream to explore, the soldiers with knives in their third eyes, the blood, and the golf course. I spent journaling time writing down my associations and discovering what was represented. The life (blood) was draining from my intuition (third eye) as bandits (the wild thieves) chased me and I "soldiered" ahead on a beautifully manicured game of life – the "golf course" after having witnessed a man's murder. Though my life (blood) was beginning to make a mess by running out uncontrolled all over the beautifully kept "golf course", I soldiered ahead running from the wild thieves pursuing me. To put it succinctly, I was ignoring my intuition at the risk of my very life being stolen from me and trying to keep everything tidy in the meantime. How long could I keep running?

I was comforted when I read in Naomi Epel's *Writers Dreaming* that Isabel Allende dreamt of soldiers marching on a golf course. She, too, was unprotected. Her comment, "I come from a very strange family. With that family you don't need to invent anything. It's given to you." That comment struck me as very familiar. I was in group therapy, discovering that all families are strange. Could I forgive the strangeness of my own?

\* \* \*

I drive to the local Dairy Queen to purchase a chocolate milkshake for my mother – a treat to compensate for her pain. It is a tradition in our family. When you are ill or hurt you get a treat – used to be a pony ride, a new book, warm cashews, a puzzle, an ice cream cone, a Coca Cola. I return to Mother's side, insert the straw in the lid, and offer it to her, placing it between her lips. She does not respond.

"Mother, it's a chocolate milkshake. Just suck it through the straw."

She looks at me blankly.

I remove the lid to see if it's too thick to move through the straw. It is already liquid, having made the trip across town in my car. I look through the cabinets to find a plastic spoon. Then I attempt to feed her this treat. She doesn't want it. She turns her head away from me.

There is nothing left for me to do here. I say the Serenity Prayer over and over, silently to myself – *Lord grant me the serenity to accept the things I cannot change, the courage to change the things I can, and the wisdom to know the difference.*

She dozes and I sit beside her.

\* \* \*

The serenity prayer isn't working. My mind leaves the present and heads to the past to one of my weekly visits to Mother just months before her move into the nursing home. Rose, who lived across the street from my mother, had met me in my mother's yard to say, "I keep inviting your momma to go to garage sales with me, but she won't do it. I worry about her being all alone over here."

Oh, yeah. Bring on the guilt, I thought. Instead, I replied, "I'll ask her about that. Thanks for caring."

As soon as I entered the house, I said, "Mother, Rose just told me you keep refusing her invitations to go to garage sales. Why don't you do that? It would be fun and get you out of the house."

"I like to go places with you, not other people. Rose is recovering from breast cancer. Being with her just reminds me of my own breast cancer," she replied.

"Mother, you have been in remission for almost twenty years!"

"I knew you wouldn't understand."

I laughed to myself about the time she said to a park ranger who inquired about whether she qualified for a reduced entry rate as a senior citizen – "I'm sixty-four, not sixty-five, but do you have a discount for cancer patients? I just had a radical mastectomy."

He stood staring at her for what seemed an eternity and then said, "No ma'am. That will be the full five dollar charge."

Later that same day, I answered a knock on Mother's door to be greeted by a short, plump woman with a big smile and a new perm. "Hi, Mary," I said. "Your hair looks nice."

"I wanted to show your mom my new hairdo," she said.

"She's in the laundry room. I'll call her."

After Mary left, Mother said, "You know she has schizophrenia."

"Yes," I replied.

"I heard on the Austin news that a man with schizophrenia killed his girlfriend and her mother. Do you think I'm in danger?" she asked.

"I don't know much about the disease," I said. "I do know Mary's family sees her every day, she has a psychiatrist, and she talks about taking her medications."

"She thinks she has a boyfriend named Paul. She says he comes every night at midnight to stay with her, but he must leave before daylight. He can't be outdoors in the light." Mother said. "I know he's imaginary, but I play along to make her happy."

I looked up schizophrenia when I got home. The official diagnosis is "a type of psychosis characterized by loss of contact with environment and by disintegration of personality." That sounds a lot like what I am witnessing in the secured unit right now.

When Mother started seeing ragamuffins under her bed and birds flying in her windows, I, too, had played along to keep her happy.

Did Daddy play along to keep her happy? What happens in a marriage when Persephone remains a girl, a mother's daughter, unwilling to claim all of herself – the dark as well as the light ?

In the myth of her descent into hell and return, Persephone was attracted to and influenced by powerful personalities. Because of her strong desire to have someone take care of her, she didn't always see the consequences of her decisions. Did she want to be under the influence of a strong mother or a god-husband? I am reminded of Sylvia Plath and Anne Sexton. Their creative geniuses snuffed out by pills, booze, and an oven. Did they look for a man to be their God, as Anne Sexton so eloquently put it in her poem *Jesus Dies* – *"I want God to put His steaming arms around me and so do you. Because we are sore creatures."*

\* \* \*

I have helped Tiffany put my mother to bed. Night comes on quietly. I sit at the headboard, my mother beside me, and I welcome it.

# CHAPTER SEVEN

## I NOW PRONOUNCE YOU MAN AND WIFE

## HERA

## GODDESS OF MARRIAGE AND COMMITMENT AND PARTNER IN-POWER

*"....It hurts to thwart the reflexes of grab, of clutch,*
*to love and let go again and again.*
*It pesters to remember the lover who is not in the bed,*
*to hold back what is owed to the work*
*that gutters like a candle in a cave without air,*
*to love consciously, conscientiously,*
*concretely, constructively..."*
- Marge Piercy, from the poem *To have without holding*

# I Now Pronounce You Man and Wife

Now it is late and I decide to stay the night in Mother's house so I can go back to see her in the morning before I leave for Colorado. Today was a challenging day in the Sunset Unit. I am exhausted. I had planned to spend the night at a hotel near the Austin Airport before flying to work in Colorado, but after finding Mother in yet another emergency, I have again rearranged my life to deal with it.

When I unlock the front door of my mother's house and enter, I am met with damp, dead air. I realize I haven't been in this house in months. In the years that Mother has resided in the nursing home, I have come to stay here less and less. I turn on the lights, adjust the thermostat, and rummage through the kitchen cabinet to find something to make for dinner. I sit on the blue floral loveseat in the living room and call Larry to let him know how Mother is and what my plans are. Then I heat some Campbells's vegetarian vegetable soup into which I put a dash of chili powder. I find a diet Coke in the refrigerator and sit down at the kitchen table to eat. I hear the drip, drip, drip from the kitchen faucet. It reminds me that I really need to sell this house. Mother has been in the nursing home for four years, and she is *not* coming back to this house, even to spend one night. I can no longer delude myself.

* * *

This morning I arrived at the nursing home to discover Mother had been moved from a wheelchair to a geriatric chair. Only the most severe cases in her unit were in these gerry chairs.

I went down the hall in search of Tiffany, who was retrieving linens from a cart. "Why is Mother in *that* chair?" I inquired of Tiffany. " It's huge, bulky, and too hard to move around."

Tiffany said, "She's safer there. She was wriggling out of the wheelchair and onto the floor. We couldn't keep her in the chair. It was too dangerous."

This is another death for my mother, and I am grieving once again. She came in here walking on her own two feet. Then she needed a cane for assistance. Next, she was behind a walker. She moved into a wheelchair for a very short time, and now she is restricted to a geriatric chair.

In spite of the fact that I really like Tiffany, I feel my anger swelling. "What if she were your mother?" I bark, with an emphasis on the *your*. "Would you treat her like this?"

"My grandmother *was* in a gerry chair when she was here," Tiffany replies. "I just thought the nurses knew what was best." Her answer defuses my indignation. Tiffany and I both have had women we love be constrained.

\* \* \*

I wash my dishes and settle in for the evening. I sit in my mother's living room surrounded by artifacts of the life she created. Staring at me from the bookshelves are framed portraits of Daddy in his Navy uniform and Mother in an ecru satin blouse. He was thirty-five at the time and she was twenty.

Mother married a man almost a generation older and was forever resisting the position that automatically put her in. Theirs was a fiery relationship punctuated with open conflict and occasional absences. Who were these two individuals who came together in marriage?

I thumb through one of Mother's many scrapbooks as if trying to reconstruct them from something as simple as black and white photographs. In them are shadows of this god-like, complex person my mother once was to me.

\* \* \*

The goddess Hera reigned in my parents' marriage. Mother's value of hierarchical, aristocratic beliefs and family and social responsibility were alive and well when she spent Sundays at my daddy's family home. Like Hera, Mother believed that *who* you married was very important. She valued the perceived wealth and possessions she beheld here. She was not alone in this way of thinking. It was the Industrial Age where women waited for men to come home from war, get a job, marry, build a house, and create a family with them. Hera's troubled marriage to Zeus is the epitome of an uneasy uniting of patriarchal warrior tribes and matriarchal cults. She should have paid attention to the shoes. Quoting her Aunt Tereza, Clarissa Pinkola Estes says, *"Look at your shoes, and be thankful they are plain…for one has to live very carefully if one's shoes are too red."* Hera, a daughter of the land, indigenous, married Zeus, the sky god. I think of the shoes worn by women in my maternal and paternal families. As much as my mother envied the shoes worn by the women in my father's family, she felt safer in her plain shoes. Mother was a widow when she purchased her first red shoes. Just now, for no reason I can fathom, I need to find them.

* * *

When my paternal extended family gathered for holidays or Sunday dinners, I was as interested in what some of the women wore as I was in the food on the mahogany marble-topped buffet in the big dining room. Though these women were "dressed to the hilt" from head to toe, it was the shoes that fascinated me.

*I watched my Aunt Benelle glide into the room on thin-soled leather sandals in the summer. It appeared to me she never wore the same pair twice. She wore buttery yellow sandals to my daddy's June birthday party, red, white, and blue sling backs to the Fourth of July celebration, hot pink bejeweled flats to a watermelon feast in August. In my opinion she had the best shoes of anyone I knew, and they always matched her outfit. Even though her cousins, Evelyn and Lucille, had a wardrobe of shoes to rival Aunt Benelle's, she won the foot fashion award every time. When I inquired as to why Momma didn't have shoes like that, she said, "Both of your daddy's sisters, Thelma and Benelle, work and make their own money. They buy what they want. If you want to choose what you buy, you better be able to make your own money."*

*After dinner, the men, wearing boots, headed to the cattle pasture with their cigars and the women drifted off to the Adirondack chairs on the big front porch, and the talk turned from politics and religion to where their shoes were purchased, what brand they were, and how hard it was to find a size eight quadruple A.*

*I sat on the porch steps and listened to the women talking, dreaming of the day when I could wear such shoes. I was fascinated with shoes, having just spent a year in corrective brown oxfords due to my bout with polio. When I got bored listening to the fashion conversation, I was grateful for my sturdy* shoes that took me through the fields to the cattle pasture in search of my daddy.

At my maternal family gatherings the shoes the women wore were durable, certainly not the focus of conversation and adulation. My grandma had tiny feet to match her four-foot eleven- inch height. She was just happy to find shoes that fit. Hers were black lace-ups with a perforated design on the toe and a substantial heel. Lots of times, after hours in the kitchen preparing the favorite dishes of her tribe using no "receipts," as she called recipes, grandma would have on her navy blue or maroon felt house shoes with her hose rolled around her ankles – definitely not a fashion statement.

The only maternal aunt whose shoes I remember was an in-law with a desire to make sure "kids know their place." I thought she was glamorous as she teetered in on her spiked heels in her tight skirt and chided Grandma for "spoiling" us. Grandma just laughed and went to the swing on the back porch to join Nora, the Negro lady who helped her with cleaning and dish washing at big family gatherings. Nora took a "breather" to dip a little snuff and catch up on the latest gossip with Grandma who was always up to date from visiting with her many friends who dropped by for coffee most afternoons on their way to town.

The rest of the family was still sitting at the food-laden round oak table in the living room or at the plank table in the kitchen, deciding if they'd have seconds of the fried chicken or brisket. If it was Sunday or a holiday Momma usually had on her one pair of Sunday shoes which Daddy had picked out. If it was spring and summer, she wore a pair of black patent leather high-heeled pumps with the toe out, and in fall and winter, a pair of black kid high-heeled pumps with the toe in.

Momma loved dressing up. She loved being called a lady.

\* \* \*

The goddess of marriage is Hera. Her name is thought to mean Great Lady. Hera, more than any other goddess, is seen as having distinctive positive and negative traits. She can be seen as a lovely and devoted wife, loyal and committed to her husband, or a jealous and vindictive shrew, bent on revenge. When her husband, Zeus, was unfaithful, she directed her rage at Zeus' other women or at the children he fathered, not at him, on whom she was emotionally dependent. Hera creates a compelling desire for marriage itself. Hera wants to be a Mrs. and to have what she associates with the potential husband – the *things* he brings with him to the marriage.

One memorable moment in my childhood was when Momma received a letter from one of Daddy's relatives addressed to her as Charlyne Brothers, no Mrs. in front. "I'm not some common woman. I'm Eddie's wife. How dare she address a letter to me as if I'm not a lady. Anyone with the least bit of common sense knows you don't send a letter addressed like this!"

Her Hera was out in full force. Hera was at home in the South where being a wife was a kind of entitlement of respect, and where woman, lady, and girl all had distinctively different meanings. It was like osmosis, learning that *lady* was a respectable married female; *girl* was a female child, virgin female, or the female help; and *woman* was an unmarried, non-virginal female. It was the South's own caste system for women.

\* \* \*

As I remember the shoes, I am reminded of what my mother associated with Daddy. She saw the handsome, self-assured man who'd just been discharged from the Navy, the big house in the country in which he had been raised, the educated, working sisters he respected, the family history that intrigued her, and the wealth of experiences he had to share. She believed he would provide her with the love and security and stability she desired. She didn't see a thirty-six year old man who liked to date, dance, and drink, had never been married, owned no property, and had had a variety of jobs - cattle driver, ranch hand, auctioneer, wild catter/oil well driller, and Navy man. He'd passed a civil service exam and been offered a job at the local post office, but he turned it down, saying, "That kind of job is too confining for me. I'd go nuts shut up inside all day."

My mother wasn't alone in her projections. Carl Jung's work proposes that the first six months of most romances is laden with projection. Hera women project an image of an idealized husband onto a man and become hypercritical and angry when he doesn't live up to the ideal.

\* \* \*

I want to see if I can find those red shoes. Mother might have saved them. If they are still in good shape, I'll wear them. Those shoes were purchased to wear to a Brothers family reunion the summer after Daddy died. They were red leather with a wooden wedge and the toe out. She was only fifty-five, and she was thinner than she'd ever been in her life. She wore those shoes with shiny red-and-white-striped slacks and a ruffly white voile blouse. I thought she looked beautiful that day.

I get up to search the four small rooms my mother lived in for the five years after she retired and before she entered the nursing home. It was important for her to own her home, though she had modest resources - - Daddy's small social security check *and* savings she had acquired after years of caring for children and selling her larger home. When these savings were depleted she worried about money. The house, I can see, needs a lot of repairs after sitting unoccupied for three years. Under the bed are two long, flat storage containers *and* a lot of dust bunnies. I pop the lids off and in one box I discover an array of fabric remnants, many of which I recognize from clothes she'd made for herself or me or my kids through the years. She always said she might make a quilt of those remnants. There were also many pairs of panty hose. What was she planning to do with those? In the other container I find sweaters and pajamas and flannel nightgowns. No red shoes.

There is a box marked *keepsakes* in the back of her extra closet. I pull it out, remove the worn masking tape that binds it, and discover an old scrapbook with pages where pictures have been removed. I wonder what pictures she didn't want me to see. There are letters and cards from me and my brother, Bobby, to her and Daddy. There are cards from Jeff, Whitney, and Brooke, the grandchildren, addressed to her. I sit on the floor surrounded by our words of love and kindness sent to commemorate birthdays, Christmas, Mother's Day, Father's Day....but find no red shoes.

I am reminded as I search the house that Daddy did not leave a pension or savings. Life with him was feast or famine. When he was making money, he spent it. When he wasn't making it, he expected us to understand. I can still hear him say during those times, "We're little rich, right now."

Those little rich times increased as I became a teenager and they provided momentum for Mother. She went into high gear, making the most of the little we had. We chopped down our Christmas tree in an uncle's pasture instead of buying one. She sewed us new clothes that looked like the ones in the stores. She had a reason to look for work. She was empowered by my father's failure to provide. Mother, like Hera, attempted to psychologically slay her husband and end her role as wife by destroying him as husband, lover, and supporter of her family in her own mind.

During those times, he would leave us on Sunday night to work in another town all week, and he would return on Friday night. Sometimes I heard Mother accuse him of having another life in another town.

I look at the clock. It's late. I need to get some sleep. I'll look for the red shoes another time.

\* \* \*

A Hera woman is attracted to a man who is confident and accomplished. She is not fascinated by the long-suffering types. However, just as Hera was drawn to Zeus' appearance as a shivering bird who turned into a god, a Hera woman can also be drawn to men with a combination of boyish charm and take-charge manliness. When the boyish charm leads to infidelities, the Hera woman will not understand why she was wrong in assessing her choice, why she saw only the exterior and not the interior man.

Mother had a conflicted relationship with Hera's qualities. She wanted to be part of a marriage partnership that was a powerful union between two individuals committed to the fulfillment of each other, but she often struggled to assert herself in an effort to have some power.

She'd already experienced one divorce and she was not going to have another. Hera women see marriage as a source of identity and well-being. If the husband divorces her, the psychological wound is crushing, and the denial can come close to delusional.

"I want to buy my own groceries," Mother said every week as Daddy carried in bags full of food and household items he'd purchased. Her frustration grew and her voice got louder and shriller as week after week her request was ignored.

"I'm going to work so I can have money of my own," Mother declared when I became a teenager. "Then I'll be able to buy my own groceries

119

and plan my own meals. We eat what you like whether we want to or not," she continued.

"No wife of mine is going to work. People will think I can't support my own family if you start working," Daddy answered.

"Some of my friends work. More and more women are doing it now," Mother persisted.

"You're not other women. You're my wife," Daddy replied.

"I know I'm your wife. I'll do something that doesn't interfere with taking care of you and the house and the kids," she promised.

She started a child care business in our home, against my daddy's wishes and without his blessing. She was happy. Each morning she greeted the parents who dropped off their children, and each afternoon she gave them a verbal report of what the kids had learned that day. She took pride in being a teacher to these little ones in her care, not just a sitter. Before long, she had a waiting list of people who wanted her services. Word had traveled and she was elated. At supper each evening, she told stories of her successes. Daddy started looking for a new job in a different town. Mother gave notice to her clients after just a year of having her own business. We moved.

Mother didn't work the next year. However, undeterred, she found a job the year after. She never quit work again. Until she retired at seventy-eight.

\* \* \*.

I get ready for bed. I have work to do myself after I see Mother in the morning. I'm driving to the Austin airport to catch a plane to Colorado, where I am to facilitate an Executive Leadership Retreat for a healthcare corporation. I'll be gone several days. Being away makes me nervous, as if I could do anything here anyway.

I awaken early so I can arrive at the nursing home in time to feed my mother her break-fast before I leave. When I arrive, she already has her plastic tray with scrambled eggs, toast, cereal, milk, orange juice, and coffee sitting untouched in front of her. Her thin face is expressionless. I wince at the sight of it. I kiss her cheek, pull up a chair beside her, and sit down. I begin to feed her. She eats everything I offer to her.

"You have an appetite," I say. "That's good."

She doesn't say anything. I feel sad. I miss her words, her stories, her comments. That surprises me. So many times in my life, I wanted her to be quiet.

\* \* \*

It seemed to me, growing up, that my parents fought a lot.

Actually though, I rarely heard Daddy say anything argumentative. In the mornings, he sat at the head of the table, newspaper in hand, sipping his black coffee, waiting while Momma fixed the breakfast she would serve to him and Bobby and me. After work, he came home, bathed, dressed in the clean, starched, and ironed clothes Momma had prepared, and sat down to the supper she had cooked. At meals he talked about his day, the men at work, what President Eisenhower or President Kennedy should do, something he'd heard about a church deacon....He asked us what we'd learned at school. Then he read or wrote letters to his family members at the table while he drank iced tea with lots of sugar. Some nights we'd all go to the drive-in movie or walk to the theater downtown. Momma and Daddy loved the movies. After we had a television, he took his iced tea to the extra room where he and Momma would sit on the daybed side-by-side to watch *Ed Sullivan*, *Perry Mason*, *Gunsmoke*, the news, or whatever else caught his attention. At ten or so, he returned to the kitchen for a snack - - usually a bowl of cornflakes and milk with lots of sugar. When we were little, we'd join him for this snack and then head to bed where he'd tuck us in and say The Lord's Prayer with us. When we were older and in our rooms alone, he'd demand the lights be turned out by 10:30.

When Momma was mad, she yelled and cups or plates or vases flew. We would be sitting at the table enjoying her smothered steak and parsley potatoes, and she would erupt!

"I'm not your slave, Eddie Brothers. I need to get away from this house. Give me some gas money so I can take the car tomorrow and go visit my momma. The car is almost empty and you didn't leave me any money today. I know what you're up to. You can't keep me captive here."

She'd leave the table in a huff. We three would sit there in silence. Uneaten food congealed on our plates getting cold. Daddy would interrupt the silence saying, "Don't worry. Your momma's just upset. She'll be fine in a little while. Finish up your supper."

Mostly I remember Bobby going out to play with his dog and me leaving my supper right where it was and going to my room while Daddy sat at the table. He seemed to know she'd be back to clean up the kitchen.

*   *   *

When Hera doesn't marry the heroic man who she imagined would create wealth and position and power for her, she reacts in one of two ways. She might manipulate him from behind the scenes, plan his every move, and make sure he moves forward in the world. Or, she nags her husband, punishes her children, and complains to her friends and family. This is the Zeus and Hera dynamic. It is the woman's protest against her husband's denying her any power. Hera wants to be out in the world where things are happening, and she hates her husband or anyone else's for keeping her from that world. She is jealous of the freedom that her husband and other men have in the world.

*   *   *

As I board the plane for my flight to Denver, I think about my mother's thrill when she flew the first time. Her first flight was to Denver, where I'd moved months earlier. I met her at the gate. It seemed her whole face was a smile. She hugged me and said, "I think your Daddy would have loved to fly. He never got the chance." At this time Daddy had been dead for nine years. She was still imagining what life would have been like were he here. That kind of thinking always caught me off guard because of, what seemed to me, her former constant striving to be free of his constraints.

"It just goes to show," as she'd often say, "you never know what goes on in a marriage. Only the two people involved know that."

I find my seat on the aisle, my preference. I don't like the confinement of a window or middle seat. You have to ask people to get up and let you out. I'd rather give up the view and have my freedom of movement. I stand for the couple in the seats beside me. I pull out my briefcase from under the seat in front of me and remove the folder which holds my retreat plans and my City Council packet. I'll review the retreat materials on the flight out and the City Council packet on the flight back. That is my intention. I can't waste a minute of my valuable time. Then I overhear my seatmates talking about the cruise from which they are returning, and their comments take me right back to the nursing home where I observed a married couple at dinner and listened to their conversation last night.

* * *

Mother was dozing throughout dinner and I watched Mr. and Mrs. Ledford, the only married couple in residence in the secured unit. They had moved in the week before, shared a room and dressed up for meals. Mr. Ledford wore a tie with his dress shirt, and Mrs. Ledford wore a scarf around her neck, bracelets, and smelled like she had just sprayed on cologne from head to toe.

"Daddy," Mrs. Ledford said, "can you believe what a lovely dinner we have been served? I know you will especially enjoy the chocolate mousse we are having for dessert."

I took the plastic lid from the tiny plastic bowl on my mother's plate to see if she, too, had chocolate mousse for dessert. It looked like Jello pudding to me. I was intrigued by this woman's view of the world.

"Mother," Mr. Ledford replied, "I am sure it cannot hold a candle to the one you make. It *is* my favorite dessert, you know."

"Daddy," I know that. "I am so glad they made it for you. I am particularly relishing this vegetable medley," she said as she forked up what looked like Bird's Eye frozen mixed vegetables. "What is your pleasure after dinner? Would you like to go for a stroll? The weather is lovely."

"Mother, that sounds like a nice diversion. I'm a little tired of staying indoors. A walk outside sounds delightful."

To the nurse's aide, Tiffany, I said, "They sound like they're on a cruise ship. I love it. They're making the most of this situation. I bet they've been like that always."

Tiffany replies, "He was my world history teacher in high school. He was always polite and kind. His class was so organized. His wife brought him his lunch to school every day."

I asked Tiffany, "Do the Ledfords have children?"

"Yes, two sons," she replied. "They haven't been here much."

To myself I think, that's another kind of marriage than the one I saw growing up.

\* \* \*

On the airplane, instead of studying my retreat plans or my City Council packet, I am wondering - is there passion in a marriage where the partners call each other Mother and Daddy?

I had recently been rereading Jennifer and Roger Woolger's *The Goddess Within*. I think about how Hera sees marriage as an institution that has little to do with love or passion. She leaves that to Aphrodite. For all its limitations, Hera is attracted to marriage because it embodies her instinct to be mated, to partner a man. Hera's wound is the pain of powerlessness. She is jealous of the freedom her husband has to be a moving force in the world. Goddess research reveals that more marriages suffer and more families are bullied by unfulfilled and injured Heras than by any other goddess type

Hera's children are never good enough, and so she directs them inappropriately to careers she herself should have followed. She positions them to feel the kind of failure by which she is eternally tormented. Jennifer and Roger Woolger report that a whole generation of women born in the 1920's and 1930's are Heras trying to create the *Father Knows Best* world of the 1940's and 1950's. It is a generational theme – alienated daughters of frustrated Heras trying to break free of inhibiting patterns of womanhood their mothers were sold. These daughters are women whose mothers' needs and fears dominated them. They are among the generations of unmothered women beginning in the Industrial Revolution to be cut off from the land, the ground of their feminine being. They have learned to substitute masculine values of power, perfection, and success. Marion Woodman, a Jungian analyst, says these women turn to the father principle for mothering and find nourishment in the ideals of the spirit and mind – morality, law, justice, duty, fidelity, tradition.

This definition resonates with me – I have spent a lifetime seeking sustenance from my work. I have relished self-employment, designing and selling programs, traveling the world consulting, and feeling a sense of accomplishment that I could support myself and my three children. *I am the woman my mother wanted to be. I am living the life of a woman whose mind is gone and who sits in a wheelchair in a locked up facility, my mother's life*

*Who* is the demented one?

\* \*

My thoughts are interrupted by the flight attendant who offers me a choice of beverages. I decline. I open my folder of retreat plans. I need to be prepared for tomorrow's strategic planning session with my client.

\* \* \*

A week later I am on a plane flying back to Texas. My days in Colorado were filled with work and short visits with my kids and grandkids. Being with my daughters and their husbands reminded me of the marriage legacy we leave our children. What effect did my three marriages have on my three children? They were two, three, and seven when their father, David, left. They were twelve, thirteen, and sixteen when I left their step-dad. They were seventeen, eighteen, and twenty-one when I married Larry.

I sit here on the plane home and recall that Mother hadn't wanted to attend Larry's and my wedding - my third wedding. I called to ask her to be there and she replied, "I've already been to two of your weddings. I don't think I need to be present for a third."

"Please. You always said third time's a charm," I cajoled her. "I already mailed you a plane ticket. It would mean a lot to Larry and me if you'd come. It's his third too, and all his family is coming."

She showed up, prepared food for the reception, but all the photographs show her standing a distance apart from the rest of us, never a smile.

At the time, the fact of my mother's divorce announcement had not surfaced in my conscious mind. I was still living under the illusion that she had been married only once, and that she thought I was a huge disappointment to her because I was a woman who couldn't stay married. To add to her humiliation, I insisted on being married in a church all three times. Only " 'trash' would do that" she exclaimed to me! She must have agreed with Oscar Wilde that *one divorce may be regarded as misfortune, but two begins to smack of carelessness.*

My mother, like Hera, believed that once a woman was married she was meant to stay that way for better or worse. A Hera woman is willing to endure bad treatment because she is married at her core. There may be disappointment and pain, but it is the price to be paid for maintaining the appearance.

* * *

I arrive at the nursing home to discover that Mother has suffered another indignity and more pain. Mother had been moved from the secured unit to a room in the main nursing home facility. I walked in to see her curled into a fetal position and heard her whimpering. She and her roommate, Louise, a woman who had also been in the secured unit, had both been moved several days ago. The smell of urine saturated the air, and I gagged upon entering. In spite of the adult diaper Mother was wearing, her gown and sheet were wet. I found a clean gown and a fresh diaper and discovered sores on her buttocks when I changed her. This was a first in my experience at the home. She had obviously been forgotten in this room, as had Louise, who was also lying on a soaking sheet. Neither one of them could speak words, only mutters and groans. No one had checked on them in some time.

My stomach clenched, my shoulders tightened, I could feel the anger surging in my body. I lifted my ninety-pound mother into a gerry chair, and pushing her in front of me, I steered her toward the administrator's office. When we arrived at the door, it was closed.

I turned toward the central nurses' station, a round island hub in the middle of a circular space with halls, like spokes, leading off in five directions. Several women in green or pink or blue scrubs were seated at the desk space inside the circle. They continued to write or talk on the phone, or to each other, as I stood waiting, beside my mother's parked chair, to be acknowledged. When no one looked up, I demanded in raised voice, "Where can I find the administrator? I need to talk with her."

"She's not here right now. Can someone else help you?" a middle-age woman I didn't recognize asked me.

"Is the assistant administrator or the social worker here?" I inquired.

"I'll page Tenley for you."

"Thanks."

I was not looking forward to talking with Tenley. We do not communicate easily with one another. I like to talk with Denise, the Administrator who followed Ross. I find Denise to be direct and informed. She is a registered nurse, in her fifties, who will admit when she makes a mistake and will tell me what she thinks whether I like it or not. We have had conflicts, but we understand one another and will talk an issue through until it is resolved. She sees nuances and realizes people are more than their diagnosis.

Tenley is a *follow the rules no matter what* kind of person. She sees things in black and white. I have surmised that she likes hierarchical power, having a title. Her office wall is lined with certificates announcing her various accomplishments. She doesn't like to be questioned. I am a questioner.

There are two employees I find myself clashing with more than any others here, and Tenley is the first of them. The other is a nurses' aide, Raina. She, too, does not want to be questioned and rarely smiles or acknowledges that my mother or any other resident is a human being, not just a diagnosis. Raina is walking down the hall with Tenley.

Tenley says, "Mrs. Charles, what can I do for you?" Denise would have called me Beverly.

"Who authorized my mother's move from the secured unit?" I demanded.

"The secured unit is full. The staff there is stretched thin. Since some of the residents there, including Mrs. Brothers, are no longer security risks, we decided to move them out on the main floor," Tenley explained.

"By *no longer security risks*, I assume you mean, *can no longer walk or talk*," I said.

"That's right," Tenley replied.

"No one asked my permission or even informed me of this move," I said, "and I am not accepting it. My mother has sores and was completely drenched in her own urine when I arrived today. *And* her roommate, Louise, is wet also. You think just because they can't walk and talk, you can stick them in a room down some hall and forget about them. That's not acceptable."

"Dr. Robinson approved the move," Tenley stated. "If you have a problem, you can discuss it with him." I could almost hear her stamp her foot.

I looked at this thirty-something wisp of a woman, the age of my daughters, standing in front of me. She was almost gloating. She had pulled the "your mother's doctor" card on me. I realized that I had never seen her smile, not even at her own grandmother who was in the secured unit with my mother. I had fed her grandmother on numerous occasions after she could no longer feed herself. I felt rage, sorrow, pity stir in me. Who is this woman I thought? Why is she working in this place? Where is her compassion?

I was torn between wanting to hug her to me to see if she responded to affection, or wanting to slap her hard across the face to see if she could even feel pain.

Instead, I stared at Tenley, pulled out my cell phone, dialed Dr. Robinson's number, which I knew by heart, and said to his receptionist, "Carolyn, this is Beverly Charles, Mrs. Brothers' daughter, and I am here with Tenley at Comfort Care. She has just informed me that Dr. Robinson authorized my mother's move from the secured unit to the main floor without my approval. My mother's buttocks are covered with sores and I arrived today to find her soaking wet in her bed, whimpering. I find this unacceptable, and I consider this an emergency, so I would like to talk with him immediately."

"He's with a patient right now. I will slip him a note and he will call you in just a few minutes."

This wasn't the first time I'd had to ask for Dr. Robinson's intervention in a situation here at Comfort Care. I trusted him to respond in a caring way.

I hung up and said to Tenley, "Dr. Robinson will call in just a few minutes. Should we stand here or go to your office and wait?" Then the phone rang.

"Beverly, this is Dr. Robinson. I hear there's a problem with your mother's care. Besides being your mother's doctor, I'm on the Comfort Care Board of Directors, and I want to assure you that we are addressing a number of concerns there right now. How can I help you?"

I repeated the description of how I'd found my mother and questioned the decision to move her, requesting, "Please instruct Tenley to move my mother back to the secured unit today. I also want to let you know I'll be calling the state's Ombudsman line again to report the situation in which I found my mother and Louise."

"I understand. I'd do the same for my mother. I'm sorry your mother's had this experience. I'll make a report to the Board also. Now, if you'll put Tenley on the phone, I'll make sure she arranges for your mother's move."

"Thank you so much," I replied. "Your prompt response to this means more than you can know."

I handed my cell phone to Tenley. She turned away from me. I couldn't see her face. She talked in a whisper. She closed my phone, handed it to me, and said, "I'll have to find a room for your mother in the secured unit today. I'll have someone move her things. Do you want to wait here or in her room?"

"I think we'll wait in the living room of the secured unit by the window. She likes to look out at the courtyard."

In hours she is back in her bed by the window in the room she's occupied for years, and I am by her side, to kiss her forehead, pull up a chair, and take her hand in mine. She looks through me. I have not been here for days, and she is so diminished by this move and its injuring after effects. I don't know how long I've been sitting here without her acknowledgement, but I need to leave. How can I watch my mother lie here bound to a chair, speechless – she, who desired above all else the power of sovereignty – the right to exercise her own will?

\* \* \*

I have been at my mother's side for hours and I cannot wait to exit. I call Larry from the car to tell him I am on my way home. I turn on NPR to distract myself from the many thoughts whirling around inside my skull. Even *Fresh Air* can't keep the cogitations at bay.

Mother married into an American history of *coverture* where upon marriage the wife is enveloped by her husband, forfeiting legal rights and property ownership. As late as the 1970's and 1980's, depending on what part of the United States you resided in, a single or married woman still had difficulty opening a bank account or securing a loan on her own. When the minister announced, "I now pronounce you man and wife," it meant the woman gave up her womanhood for the role of wife. The man was still a man.

Part of Mother's legacy to me was expressed in my refusal in 1964 to use the "obey" in my wedding vows, and a desire to create with my husband-to-be our *own* vows. That decision was only the beginning of many discoveries related to my marriage legacy, a heritage unearthed gradually through the years of living. It's an anthropological study of sorts, spotting and shining the light on the many marriages in my ancestral line that preceded my own. It is a marital relationship lineage. I have discovered I am from strong hard-working women with big imaginations who married dreamy, philosophical men who expressed impassioned opinions about politics, religion, and the meaning of life while trying to "make a living." I am from relationships where raised voices and the conflict that arises among differences is the norm for the women and quiet reserve followed by occasional disappearance, literally or figuratively, is the norm of the men.

The blood of my ancestors flows through my veins and also activates my imagination in regard to what it means to be a wife or a husband. Daddy was cool and collected, not easily ruffled. Affectionate, but not emotional. He valued rationality. His mother played the piano, organ, and violin, rested in the afternoon, read books, and wrote letters. His daddy rode horseback, supervising the hands on the cotton farm he owned and left, on occasion, for the baths and massages offered at the hot springs in Marlin. British blood flowed in his veins on both his maternal and paternal sides. An aunt once told me, "Your daddy's lineage entitles you to membership in the DAR – Daughters of the American Republic." I laughed to myself, knowing how disgusted Daddy would be by the thought of such a thing, how he warned me against joining anything that "reeked of exclusion." He was a cowboy poet at heart, tanned by the wind and sun, at home on a horse, attired in Stetson and boots, roaming free. Ironically, what he most disdained about the DAR may have been one of the things that the Hera in my mother was attracted to.

Hera women value the gentry. I once wrote a poem titled *"My Mother Was A WASP Wannabe."* Mother referred to her own bloodline as a Heinz 57 mixture – English, Irish, French, German, Scot. Her daddy was orphaned as a child, took the whip of a punishing stepfather as he worked his fields, and longed for the love of the mother who did not come to her child's defense. His mother had been orphaned at the age of thirteen aboard the ship that was carrying her with her family from

Ireland to the United States. My mother's maternal great-grandfather had immigrated from Prussia, acquiring many acres of farm land and teaching his six children the value of working hard, praying hard, building something for the generations to come, and living and dying in the same place, honored by their family, friends, and neighbors when they passed on. The women did what they were told until a time came when they stood up and talked back and the men sulked and hid and spent more time away from home.

Jung argued that our actual parents are nominal, and that our real parents are our ancestors.

Says Mary Oliver in *Long Life* - "*Along with the differences that abide in each of us, there is also in each of us the maverick, the darling stubborn one who won't listen, who insists, who chooses preference or the spirited guess over yardsticks or even history. I suspect this maverick is somewhat what the soul is, or at least that the soul lives close by and companionably with its agitating and inquiring force. And of course all of it, the differences and the maverick uprisings, are part of the richness of life. If you are too much like myself, what shall I learn of you, or you of me?*"

I feel as if I am glimpsing my mother's soul these days. I am not sitting with the mother I have so long resisted. There is nothing here to resist. Who is she? Who am I? Why are we here?

At my mother's house, I do not find Mother's red shoes. Why did I think she would keep a pair of shoes for thirty years? My mother never kept things she didn't need anymore. She passed them on to someone who might find them useful. I had hoped she'd kept them because I'd felt I needed them now, but what I'd needed was this: to remember my mother, the one who shimmered that day in her striped slacks, voile blouse, and red shoes – so alive.

* * *

I stop the car at a roadside park. At the concrete table, I sit and call to check on Mother. I request to speak to Tiffany.

"This is Beverly, Mrs. Brothers' daughter. How is she?" I ask.

"She's sleeping. She's fine. Don't worry about her," Tiffany tells me.

"Thanks," I respond.

How do I tell Tiffany what I am feeling is not worry? It is deep sorrow? I am mourning the loss of my mother, but I am also grateful for this lingering good-bye.

Mother is taking her time, dancing on the threshold between the visible and invisible worlds, dying many deaths, ensuring that I *'behold'* her. Not the roles she inhabited – daughter, wife, mother - *but the essence of her.*

# CHAPTER EIGHT

## MOTHER MARY COME TO ME

## MARY

## THE MOTHER OF GOD, COMPASSION, HER NAME IS KINDNESS

*"The word 'feminine' has very little to do with gender,
nor are women the sole custodians of femininity.
Both men and women are searching
for their pregnant virgin.
She is the part of us who is outcast,
the part who comes to consciousness
through…mining our leaden darkness
until we bring her silver out."*
from *The Pregnant Virgin*, Marion Woodman,
*Jungian analyst, lecturer, and body workshop leader*

Year Five

# Mother Mary Come To Me

I spot her in the garden department at the local Wal-Mart. She is three feet tall, dressed in a red gown, and draped in a blue cape dotted with gold stars. Her eyes cast down and her hands folded in prayer, she stands on a bed of pink and red roses, an angel peeking out from her hem, an aura of golden scalloped light encircling her. She is the Virgin de Guadalupe. I must have her for my Goddess Getaway, the name with which I have recently christened my office/writing studio. She will reign on the east wall, which has been painted saffron, beside the large wooden cross and the ceramic mask and under the drawing of the whirling dervishes, the Bulgarian Madonna and Child icon, the framed photos of the Buddhist Monks praying in the Himalayas, and the print of a winged angel carrying a small child over the darkened silhouette of a city.

I need this Mother Goddess, this being in whom one can have total trust, to be with my mother and me right now, to shepherd us through these days. I make the purchase, carry her to my car, and fasten the passenger side seatbelt around her for the journey home.

\* \* \*

In recent months, Mother is fading from me. She weighed seventy-eight pounds last week. She is so small and lies curled up in the fetal position most of the time.

Dr. Robinson told me years ago, "The time will come when your mother will no longer recognize you, no longer have the language to call you by name."

I had resisted that announcement claiming, "Not my mother! She's never missed a birthday. She's always the first to call. She likes to talk too much. She won't stop talking to me."

Months have passed with, at the most, grunts and moans from her. I yearn for the sound of her voice. I search for an old video-taped interview I did with her one Christmas. I pine for her words.

"I can't do this anymore!" I exclaim to Larry when I return home with my resin Madonna. "What kind of God takes someone in bite-sized pieces like this?"

"Mad at God, huh?" Larry asks.

"I guess so." I answer.

\* \* \*

I am reminded of a night right after David left. Jeff was seven and I heard him crying after I'd put him to bed. I went in to check on him and asked, "What's wrong?"

"If I'm angry at God, will he hurt me?" Jeff asked. " 'cause I'm mad at God for letting Daddy leave us."

I was twenty-nine years old and the only god I knew to be acceptable in my culture was the Sunday School god of my youth, a disembodied voice proclaiming laws from mountains and burning bushes, or a gentle long-haired man in a belted white robe walking on the water during storms and raising people from the dead. I had been eight years old when I'd had my first real encounter with the spiritual, and had come to know that God was very personal and real to me. I just didn't yet have the language to talk about it without raising the ire or eyebrows of those around me.

Just then Jeff and I had both needed a big lap to crawl into, a mother's reassurance that everything was going to be okay. I think I muddled through a response something like, "God loves us no matter how we feel. God is big enough to hold all our feelings." But had I really believed what I was telling my son?

For years I vacillated between falling on my knees in faith *or* making sure every detail was cared for, and that I was in total control, vigilant, lest any mishaps occur. Of course, mishaps always occurred. In one of Ram Dass' books, I read that he believed life was the curriculum and we were the students of that course of study. I latched on to that philosophy, looking for lessons in all the many challenges with which my life bombarded me – illnesses, birth defects, divorces, love affairs, rebellious teenagers, car wrecks, and work. It comforted me to see that I was learning, that this was not a life lived in vain, meaningless.

\* \* \*

I arrive on a Saturday morning, look at my mother sleeping in her geriatric chair, and know I must do something to distract myself from the pain I feel sitting beside her. I decide she needs new nightgowns, pretty pastels for spring. At the store, I look through the racks in the lingerie section, and identify several frilly, soft flowered and striped gowns. I choose size extra small and put matching socks in the basket as a finishing touch.

At the nursing home, I attempt to waken my mother to try on a gown. She lies limp in my arms. I pull her close, taking off a faded gown in exchange for this cheery yellow one.

"Momma, it's spring. I bought you a pretty yellow gown with eyelet trim around the neck. You look so pretty in yellow," I say before my voice cracks and I have to leave again.

\* \* \*

Years ago I'd gone to see Mel Gibson's film, *Passion of Christ*. I had resisted it for weeks, thinking it was too violent for my taste. Finally, intrigued by what I'd read, I went to see it. I sat in the theater, astounded by the violence perpetrated on the Christ. But, even given that, what remained with me were the scenes of Mary, His mother, walking alongside Him on the way to the cross, bearing witness to His pain. I was struck by her willingness to hold the space for His suffering. Just like she'd held the space in her womb for Him, Mary held the space for His suffering in her heart.

Isn't that what we all want, I decided – a mother to hold the space for our suffering? Wasn't that a kind of holiness all in its own?

Does God the Father imagine, I wondered? Does Mary the Mother create? Does Jesus the Son walk among us? Does the Holy Spirit, the Divine, inhabit us? Does that give us meaning?

\* \* \*

Five years, to the month, after Mother's move into the nursing home, I am on a Frontier flight from Denver to Austin with my two grandsons, Austin and Logan. They are eleven and eight, and they are fighting over the window seat trying to see what animal is on the tail of our plane. I'd picked them up on my return from an out-of-state writing conference. I hand them each a bag with the Gatorade and spiced nuts they'd chosen as snacks. Then I receive the call.

"Beverly, your mother isn't eating or drinking. She's sleeping most of the time," says Joan, a hospice nurse I've not yet met.

Mother has been under hospice care off and on for over a year. She has periods of coma-like existence, then rallies back to life. Something in the tone of Joan's voice tells me this time is different.

"I'm on a plane to Texas right now," I tell her. "I arrive at the Austin airport about two o'clock. My husband will pick me up and we'll be in Hallettsville by four or so. I'll come straight there."

My pulse has quickened, and I let out a sigh. Austin and Logan have fallen asleep with their earphones in place. I look at them, mentally making a list of what to do when we arrive – drive to Oak Meadows where Larry will stay with the boys, get my car, and go to the nursing home.

Oak Meadows is the name of the house and land we purchased with the money I inherited from my Aunt Dot and Uncle Howard, my mother's brother and sister-in-law. Oak Meadows is located in my motherland – the county where seven generations of my maternal family have lived and died. We have used it as our hurricane escape destination for a couple of years. It is a comforting place – trees, meadows, and tank and branch (Texas for pond and creek). I need comforting now. Artemis, goddess of the wilderness, lingers near in the healing nature of this setting. To all she brings a sacred connection to the elements and the mystery of being.

Larry, wearing cargo shorts, his favorite hibiscus-design polo shirt, and a beard he'd grown in the ten days I've been gone, meets us at the baggage claim area. After hugs and kisses all around, we find our bags and roll them toward the truck. I've already spoken to Larry on the phone from the plane.

We arrive at Oak Meadows, or, OM as we call it. The initials for our place in the country thrilled our yoga-practicing daughter, Whitney, who exclaimed, not without humor, "Oak Meadows, OM, God's breath, the breath of life."

At the house, Larry says, "You run on now, and the boys and I will go fish at the tank."

I am relieved. "I'll call you when I know what the situation is," I reply.

The fourteen-mile drive into town takes an eternity. On our farm to market road, I pass herds of Black Angus, Brahma, and Hereford cows. When I turn onto U.S. Highway 77, I enter a stream of truck and trailer traffic, interrupted by the occasional recreational vehicle. Someone honks and I realize I am not going the requisite seventy miles per hour. I speed up. It is a hot July day in Texas and the sun shines brightly. I stare into it, no sunglasses to protect me from the glare.

I arrive at Comfort Care, park in the almost empty parking lot, take a deep breath, and walk in. I go straight to my mother's room without stopping to talk to anyone. It is dark and stuffy. Mother is comatose, curled into the fetal position, and her skin looks almost transparent. I can see her pulse beat. Her veins are blue and show through her thin skin. I sit beside her on the bed and take her hand in mine. I am stunned and unable to move. I don't know how long I've been sitting when Raina, the nurse, saunters in. She walks straight to me, pulls me close to her in a hugging embrace, and I break into sobs. Raina, who I have judged in the past as uncaring, is caring for me. She understands my sorrow.

\* \* \*

Mary is in Mother's room. Genuine compassion gives birth to an instinctual response to do something to ease suffering. It is said that the Dalai Lama repeats this verse daily –

*As long as space remains*
*As long as sentient beings remain*
*Until then, may I too remain*
*And dispel the miseries of the world.*

Compassion is not gender specific or age specific, though many people report their own compassion increasing as they grow older.

It is challenging to bear witness to suffering without becoming impacted by it. When we look at another with empathy, or listen with empathy to another, we take their suffering into our body and soul. When what we are seeing or hearing may be beyond our own understanding, we are called on to become larger, more substantial, so that we may be capable of containing all we are seeing, hearing, and feeling. Otherwise, we are threatened by emotional woundedness or by emotional remoteness.

Mary bears witness with mercy.

\* \* \*

"Do you want me to call for the hospice nurse?" Raina inquires.

"Yes," I reply.

"I'll go do that. Do you need anything, water, coffee?" she asks.

"No thanks," I respond.

"I'll be back in a minute," Raina says as she leaves the room.

She returns with the hospice nurse, Joan. Joan radiates energy and goodwill. Her smile is kind. She is dressed up – linen suit, jewelry, heels. I imagine that she has been to church or a party today. She probably stopped what she was doing to come when they called.

"Are you okay?" Joan asks. "Would you like me to sit with you?"

"Please explain what is happening now," I say.

"Your mother has stopped eating and drinking," Joan reports as she pulls up a chair across from me and leans toward me. "She does not waken. I think she is ready to go," Joan explains. "I suggest we move her into a hospice room on another hall. It will be a private room where you and your family can be with her without much interruption. Is that what you would like?"

"Yes, thank you," I say.

"Give me a little while to arrange for this. Then I'll come back and we'll move your mother."

"Okay," I answer, all I can manage.

When she returns, I am still sitting where she left me.

"We have the room ready, and Raina and Tiffany are going to help me move your mom now," Joan tells me.

I follow their lead. They roll Mother's bed out of the secured unit, into the central hub, and then down the hall to her designated hospice room. It is a standard room with two single hospital beds, two nightstands, a chair upholstered in plastic, and a gerry chair in the corner. A curtain divides the room. Joan pulls it aside to make a single area. The half-bath door is ajar.

Mother has not stirred during this entire process.

Joan stands with her hands on her hips, "Beverly, I'm going to leave now, but I'll be checking in with the night nurse. Do you need anything before I go? We've left instructions to keep your mother comfortable by giving her something for pain, moistening her lips, and shifting her from side to side in the bed."

"No, I'll be fine," I answer.

Joan closes the door when she leaves, and I am alone with my dying mother. I look out the window and notice it is almost dark. I have been here several hours. I need to call Larry. We decide together that he does not need to bring the boys tonight.

Then I call my brother. "Bobby," I say. "Mother's passing over. Do you want to come?"

We talk and he says, "I'll come in the morning."

"Okay," I reply. Fearing she will pass before he arrives, I ask, "Why don't I hold the phone to her ear and you can tell her you love her?"

I put my cell phone to my mother's ear. I hear my brother say loving things to her, her eyes open, milky blue, and tears roll down her cheeks. I begin to cry.

This same scene is repeated as I call my children, Jeff, Whitney, and Brooke. Each of them says, "I love you, Grandma" and her eyes open and tears roll.

\* \* \*

Marion Woodman, a Jungian psychologist, says that if you *"pull in your own essence, this suffering is not meaningless. [You] trust that something new is being born from the chaos…. Conscious femininity gives us the courage to trust in the moment without knowing what the goal is."*

If our human work is to return our souls to our bodies, to return ourselves to ourselves, and overcome the human state of self-alienation, as the writer and philosopher Norman O. Brown says, then am I witnessing my mother's soul and body coming together in this moment.

I feel the presence of Mary, the Mother of God, here with us.

\* \* \*

Early in the evening, I call my cousin, Nan, while she is on her way to church. It is Sunday night. "If you need me, I'll skip church and come," she offers.

"No," I say, "I'll be fine," not wanting to interrupt her plans.

She comes to be with me, ignoring my response. I am *so* grateful to see her. Now, Nan and I sit quietly at my mother's side.

"Have you eaten?" she inquires.

The question brings me back to the present. "No, I guess I haven't."

"It's almost ten o'clock. I'll call Beep and he can bring you something. There'll be leftovers from the church supper we prepared," Nan offers.

In just minutes, Beep, Nan's nicknamed husband, comes bearing a small ice chest full of food and drink. Beep looks like a teddy bear version of Dennis Hopper. He is calm and tenderhearted. Larry and I always say, after spending any time with Beep, "If I were in a crisis, I'd want Beep there." He knows how to manage life with his down-to-earth how-to knowledge and skills, and he does it without a lot of fanfare. Beep hugs me and sits alongside Nan. They visit with me as I snack.

We make small talk. "How was church?" Nan asks Beep.

"Small crowd as usual," he replies.

"Everybody out there's getting older. No young ones to take our place," Nan responds.

"Thanks for bringing me this picnic," I say.

"No problem. We had leftovers from the church supper Nan and I put together for everyone," Beep answers.

When they leave, Nan hugs me and says, "I'll come in the morning."

I am grateful for Nan's presence. She is the rock, the anchor of our maternal extended family.

I call Larry to tell him good night, then crawl into bed with my mother.

I am nestled in with my head near her heart. I fall asleep. During the night, nurses come and go, and I get up as they change her, take her vitals, and make sure she is comfortable. Then I return to her side in the bed.

I cannot believe I am sleeping with my dying mother. The body is amazing, I think as I lie here dozing off and on. Her body carried me into this world, and now I am with her as she prepares to leave her body.

Lying here with my own mother, embodied, I drift in and out of dreams of the mothers before me, of mother earth, of the feminine. I think of myself and my wounded mother and wonder how much wounding of the feminine lies in the unconscious of all men and women?

\* \* \*

Psychological work is soul work. Marion Woodman says, "*Soul-making is constantly confronting the paradox that an eternal being is dwelling in a temporal body. That is why it suffers and learns from heart.*"

\* \* \*

Monday morning comes. Raina brings me a cup of coffee in a pink melamac mug.

"Do you need cream or sugar?" she asks.

"No, I drink it black. Thank you for thinking of me," I respond.

Raina's tenderness touches me once again.

Larry, my husband, and Austin and Logan, my grandsons, appear. We hug. The boys, Mother's great-grandsons, lean their skateboards against the wall. One of mother's nurses has brought a box of kolaches for breakfast. Larry goes for coffee and juice.

My brother Bobby and his wife, Tina, arrive. Bobby has dark hair streaked with silver and is wearing a short-sleeved summer shirt with the "tail out," as my mother would have said. Sometimes I still see the red-haired, freckle-faced boy I roamed the countryside with, playing Tarzan, Jungle Jim, or cowboys. Bobby and Tina are lean and brown from hours spent practicing yoga, tending their organic garden, and trying to get an olive grove started on their land.

I have put out a few pictures from Mother's old room – mostly of family members – and an ivy plant I'd purchased years ago to ensure she had something green in her room. I wish she had music. She loved music, but, I'm too exhausted to get the boom box from home.

A friend of many years, Mary Locke, arrives, saying, "I got off the phone with you and thought, there's no reason I can't go to be with her, so here I am."

"And I am so glad you are," I say as I embrace her.

She hands me a bouquet of flowers and I place them on the bedside stand with one of the family pictures and a Bible I'd pulled out earlier this morning . The bedside stand has become an altar of sorts, a hearth to hover round, symbolic of the need for warmth and light in our inner world as well as the outer one. Hestia, goddess of the home and hearth, is here among us.

Megan, a hospice aide, arrives to bathe and change my mother. Megan is petite, with a ring of raven-colored curls bouncing around her pretty face. She pulls the dividing curtain across to provide privacy, and she hums and sings and talks to Mother as she cares for her. "Here's some balm for you to use on your mom's lips," she instructs. "They will be dry since she's not drinking fluids. And here's a cup of ice too. You might just rub an ice cube around the rim of her mouth." The room smells of soap and talcum powder. Megan brushes Mother's silver hair and exclaims, "Don't you look pretty, Mrs. Brothers." I want to hug Megan for attending to my mother's body so lovingly. Megan is our Aphrodite.

The minister arrives. Reverend John Landau has faithfully visited my mother throughout her entire residence here. He always looks like he has given attention to his appearance. His shoes are polished, his shirt starched and ironed, and his hair freshly cut and parted. He has a gentle, warm way about him that immediately puts one at ease. He has a lankiness that is endearing. *And*, he is a Methodist minister. That means a lot to my mother who always felt Methodism was the religion of her roots.

\* \* \*

I long ago stopped attending church in the Southern Baptist denomination in which I grew up. I, like many of my generation, studied the world's religions. My roots are in Christianity, but not in the way I was originally taught. My understanding of God, the Divine, has been enhanced by Buddhist teachings, by meditation, by the idea that most Buddhists don't say, I am a Buddhist. They say, "I practice Buddhism." I've come to believe that I "practice" Christianity and I have faith that Christ's message is love. To me, keeping in mind that *I am practicing Christianity* keeps it alive and in motion. That practice has been strengthened by my openness to all faiths, the members of which desire to know the Divine.

Writers and poets like Rumi, Hafiz, Mary Oliver, John O'Donohue, Emily Dickinson, Jack Kornfield, Ram Dass, Henri Nouwen, Thomas

Moore, Annie Lamott, Parker Palmer, and David Whyte, all speak to me in voices that evoke the Divine. Yet in my darkest moments, I often return to the Bible and one of my favorite scriptures.

*"And we know that all things work together for good to them that love God, to them who are the called according to His purpose."* Romans 8:28, King James Version, or *"For I know if I believe that God is love and that God desires for me to be love too, then all that occurs in this life incarnate is to call me to more love."* Romans 8:28, Beverly Ann Charles' Life Version.

For as long as I can remember, this has been my favorite Bible verse. I memorized it from the stack of cards given me in Vacation Bible School in the fifties. The cards were a different color for each day, orange, blue, green, and so on. In my mind this verse must have been on the blue card. Why blue? Because blue always makes me slow down and think. It calms my spirit. It feeds my soul. Even as an eight year old memorizing this verse, I loved the sound of it on my tongue and the security it gave me to believe that God had a plan and that, if I believed in this plan, things would be not just okay, but good.

I have recited this verse over and over to myself in hospital corridors, funeral homes, nursing homes, churches, emergency rooms, cars, board rooms, political meetings, on river banks and sea shores, in my bed at night, and even standing in a circle at an ecumenical service in a Rocky Mountain bar.

I had looked at the liquor bottles illuminated by the sun streaming in and thanked God for the stained glass in our makeshift temple as I took my turn sharing a scripture that had been significant in my life - Romans 8:28.

Now I was reciting it to myself in my dying mother's hospice room.

\* \* \*

After the minister, John Landau, says a prayer with us, I walk him to the door and out into the hall. "John," I tell him, "Mother wanted you to be the minister for her funeral service."

"I'll be honored to do that," he replies. "I'll be stopping in each day."

"We appreciate that."

Later, there is a knock on the door. A woman, my age, introduces herself. "I'm Margaret Dusek, a hospice volunteer," she informs me. "I've been visiting your mother for months. I was thinking of her this morning, and I wanted to stop in, hold her hand, and say a rosary for her. Is that okay?"

Athena must metaphorically become a mother's daughter as well as a father's daughter. Athena is in this room now cherishing the honoring of one mother by another.

Is it okay? I want to shout, *Okay!* It is a miracle! You are bringing Mary into the room with us. Thank you! Thank you! But instead, I say, "What a lovely thing for you to do. Yes, please come in."

\* \* \*

Jeff, my son and my mother's first grandchild, arrives and greets me with an embrace that speaks volumes. Jeff has come from Austin, where he lives now. He offers a contagious calm. Jeff spent many weekends enjoying the indulgence of a grandma who let him roam the streets of downtown, swim in the San Marcos River, and feast on junk food from the Sac 'n-Pac. Jeff has taken off from his architectural day job to be here as long as we need him. His wife, Miriana, will come later. Jeff, a talented musician, has brought his acoustic guitar and plays and softly sings to his grandmother for hours on this Monday afternoon. One of his offerings is "Stairway to Heaven."

\* \* \*

When Mother and I had talked about the kind of funeral she wanted, years before her dementia set in, she'd said, "I want Jeff to play his saxophone and Michael to play the piano, and one song I want is 'When the Saints Go Marching In.'" That same day she'd informed me, as we looked at caskets, "I want a water-proof one. You know I've always been afraid of drowning." At the time, I couldn't help but laugh.

\* \* \*

Whitney, my daughter, who lives in Denver, has made arrangements to come, and Jeff will pick her up at the airport in Austin and bring her here. Todd, her husband, will fly in later. Growing up, Whitney enjoyed the same wish fulfillment from Grandma as did Jeff. For a year, as an adult, she lived in Austin and would drive over every Thursday evening to have dinner with her grandma. Now, her arrival brings a flurry of energy into the room. Though she is only five four and slender, she casts a big presence. Her long, dark, wavy hair flows down to her shoulders, her big brown eyes sparkle, and she wears a summery sun dress and gold sandals. She brushes Mother's hair, puts balm on her lips, calls her sons, Austin and Logan over to "give MeMa," their affectionate name for my mother, a kiss. Later, Whitney goes to get take-out for lunch. When she returns, she sits on Mother's bed and says, "Grandma, it's Whitney. I love you. Remember when you took me to Rio Vista to swim and bought us Payday candy bars and cokes" and "I loved coming to your house for the weekend. You'd make homemade mac and cheese and we'd watch 'Love Boat' and 'The Dukes of Hazzard'?"

Brooke, my youngest daughter, and her husband, Phil, are enroute, driving from Colorado. Brooke, too, was spoiled by Grandma. Like any kid, she loved it at the time. As an adult she'd once remarked, "Because of my disability, Grandma let me get away with too much, so I think it's better that you were stricter."

Brooke and Phil arrive road-weary and apologetic for not being here sooner. I assure them Grandma knows they came as quickly as possible. Brooke has giant blue eyes with long dark lashes. She sits in her wheelchair, looks up at me, teary, and says, "I just wanted to get here as soon as possible to be here for you. I can't believe we had to have car trouble. What do you need us to do?"

Phil apologizes for not wanting to be in the hospice room. "It just reminds me too much of my dad's illness and death," he says. "I can stay outside with Austin and Logan and give them time to skateboard and play."

I am just thankful they are all here. I am feeling blessed by the presence of my three children, and so conscious of their loving ways. There is an almost palpable sweetness here among us.

Throughout the week, we are joined by family and friends. At night, various ones of us gather around a big table at a local Mexican restaurant, and for a little while, we all bask in the joy of just being here, an extended family, enjoying our supper together.

My children are adults, living lives of their own, and Demeter, goddess of motherhood, is here to remind me that the transitions from maiden to mother to crone are natural. Spiritual resources are needed to assist mother and child in navigating the forks in the road.

* * *

Forks in the road offer us choices. Throughout our lives we have opportunities to bring light to our darkness, consciousness to our unconsciousness, unity to our separateness. Mary is there to help us. She is the representation of the feminine ascension to heaven, the link between heaven and earth, between the spiritual and the material and between the light and the darkness.

* * *

Monday night I fell and broke my right wrist. After twenty-four hours in my mother's hospice room, numerous interactions with family and friends, and an encounter with my own sibling jealousy, I'd gone to Oak Meadows to take a shower, change clothes, and return to Mother's side. I was distracted and did not pay attention when I walked down the steps.

I was now wearing a cast that covered my hand and arm, just below my knuckles to just below my elbow, and rendered me helpless to do a number of things I'd always taken for granted as a right-handed person. The right side of the body is associated with the left-brain, the masculine, the take-charge, can-do part of us. Here I was, my wounded masculine needing to surrender to the feminine, the receptive, space-offering, waiting part of us.

I stayed at my mother's side from Sunday to Thursday with only breaks for a visit to the ER, showers, changes of clothes, and evening meals. I spent the night there with her when everyone else left.

Wednesday, about midnight, I was awakened by Larry. I was surprised to see him. He said, "I woke up and thought, if this were my mom, you'd be here with me, and I just knew I had to come in and be with you tonight." I teared up, and he held me close to him. Larry's mother, diagnosed with Alzheimer's years before, was in a care facility in Colorado Springs. Larry's brother, Ken, was her primary care taker, and we had been visiting her there every few months for several years.

"Who'd have thought both of our mothers would spend the end of their lives without their minds?" Larry asked.

* * *

Blaise Pascal may have described dementia perfectly in his *Pensees*, 131, when he said, *"Nothing is so unbearable to a man as to be completely at rest, without passions, without business, without diversion, without study. He then feels his nothingness, his falseness, his weakness, his emptiness...."* It could also describe the person who sits with the demented one.

Mother is offering me a final lesson before she leaves. These five years with her in her increasing dementia, and these four days with her in hospice care are a benefaction. This time with her has been sacred. I have looked directly at my own inner emptiness and sat with it in awe. I have examined my fear of what is above and beyond and inside. I have embraced the darkness. Persephone, the goddess of the underworld, is surely in the corner appreciating the circuitous route taken to arrive at this place of compassion and imagination, with access to the collective unconscious.

Hera is here also, in our creating space to allow us to come into our own.

\* \* \*

I watched, *The Secret Life of Bees* again recently and ran for a pen and paper to write down a line – "Mary will rise, and when she does she will not go up into the sky but further inside me," says Lily, the main character, who is in search of her mother, a mother, *the* mother.

\* \* \*

In my mother's room, Larry reclines in the gerry chair with a pillow and blanket. I stretch out on the single bed. At three a.m. the nurse wakens us. "You told me to alert you if anything changed," she says. "Your mother's breaths are farther apart, and her legs are purplish. She's getting ready to go."

Larry and I move first toward each other, and then we go to Mother. I sit down on her left side as close as I can get to her, hold her hand and put my cheek to her cheek. Larry stands on her right side and takes her hand in his. I kiss her softly, repeatedly.

Mother used to ask me, "Why can't someone just come and tell me what is on the other side?"

I'd chuckled when she said it, so often that one time I'd gone in search of a passage from Alice Walker's, *The Color Purple*, to read to her -"*Here's the thing, say Shug. The thing I believe. God is inside you and inside everybody else. You come into the world with God. But only them that search for it inside find it. And sometimes it just manifest itself even if you not looking, or don't know what you look for. Trouble do it for most folks, I think. Sorrow, lord. Feeling like shit. It? I ast. Yeah, It. God ain't a he or a she, but a It. But what do it look like? I ast. Don't look like nothing, she say. It ain't a picture show. It ain't something you can look at apart from anything else, including yourself. I believe God is everything, say Shug. Everything that is or ever was or ever will be. And when you can feel that, and be happy to feel that, you've found it.*"

Mother has caused me to wonder if, throughout our lives, someone or something *is* telling us what is on the other side, and on this side too, if we will just listen and allow it to be there – love.

In the last few years, I have held her hand, kissed her, and said to her my goodbye words, every time I visited, "Mother, love is on the other side. Love is on this side. Love is everywhere. Surrender to the love."

But this time as I whisper these words into her ear, I hear her take a last deep breath, and I know she has taken leave. Her soul has bid farewell to her body. It is so still in this dimly lit room. Larry, his left hand in her right hand, me, my right hand in her left hand, reach across her tiny body and clasp each other's outstretched hand.

I imagine her being carried on the wings of angels. Tears roll down my cheeks as I witness my mother peacefully surrender to *the love* in my presence.

# EPILOGUE OR AFTERWORD

*"How do you tell the story of your life –*
*of how you were born, and the world you were born into,*
*and the world that was born into you?*
from *The Sacred Journey* by Frederick Buechner

# EPILOGUE

At Mother's funeral, there was scripture, prayer, laughter, stories, and testimony. "When the Saints Go Marching In" was played as she desired – Jeff on the saxophone and Michael on the piano. Her nephews were pallbearers, as she'd requested. Lunch, in the church fellowship hall, followed the burial. Family groupings were photographed under big live oak trees on the church lawn. The sun shone brightly.

I couldn't help but recall a family reunion a few years ago when my cousin, Charles, looked at his parents, my mother, and our aunt and uncle, all sitting together at a table under the covered patio, eating and visiting, and remarked, "Life's a conveyor belt and they're all at the end, and we are right behind them." We cousins all laughed.

Two months after Mother passed over, Larry and I had to evacuate our island home because of the threat of Hurricane Ike. My broken wrist was out of the cast, but almost useless, and I was going to physical therapy to improve its strength and mobility. We finished the evacuation and drove to our escape house, only to find it, too, was under evacuation notice due to Ike's wide path across Texas. Standing in the yard, picking up lawn furniture, yard lights, and garden hoses (which can become destructive missiles in hurricane force winds), my wrist throbbing, dark coming quickly, I began to sob uncontrollably.

All the unshed tears of weeks or months or years came flooding out. I sat down on the ground and gave myself over to the grief. Loss and possible loss surrounded me. My mother and mother earth conspired to remind me of what this human life brings with it - mortality, impermanence, vulnerability, defenselessness. Bob Dylan's words sang in my ears, *"When you get yesterday, today, and tomorrow in the same room, no telling what can happen."*

Larry, sweaty and windblown, helpless to do anything in the face of all my sorrow, said, "I think you're exhausted. We've almost got it all put away. I can finish up now. Go on in."

I got up, walked into the house, undressed, took a hot bath, and went to sleep.

That night, I awoke from a dream about my mother. In the dream, she is visiting the house where Larry and I are living, an unfamiliar house, one that we have not lived in for very long. It is evening, and we are sitting downstairs. I realize that she has been upstairs for some time and that I should check on her. I ascend the stairs, knock on the bedroom door, hear her say, "Come in," and I enter the room.

She is standing in front of a free-standing full-length mirror, completely naked. Her head is bald and covered with a pale blue embroidery-like transfer design of flowers, vines, and small birds. It is stunning. She does not turn to look at me. We can see one another in the mirror. I ask if she wants to join Larry and me downstairs, and she declines. Then I inquire as to whether or not she needs any help in preparing for bed.

"No, I'm fine," she replies.

The dream left me with a feeling of contentment. I took it as a message from her to me that we had truly seen one another in all our nakedness, our vulnerability. I further surmised that we each recognized the divine feminine in the other, and that we accepted one another just as we had been — two women in the world, learning to trust and embrace the feminine divine.

\* \* \*

I remembered how she enjoyed telling me the story of my birth. On my birthday, she was always the first to call with my birth story, saying, "Happy birthday, Beverly Ann. When you were born my momma said, 'It's a girl — just what I wanted.' She'd made a pink layette and had it all ready for you. She was so sure I'd have a girl. You know what they say, 'A son is a son until he takes a wife. A daughter is a daughter for all of your life.' "

\* \* \*

Six months after Mother's passing, I heard on NPR that a psychologist named D.W. Winnicott had developed the concept of the "good-enough mother," the mother who expresses enough love to nurture a child without damaging him or her, even though the mother may mix her expressions of love with a certain amount of neurosis.

Recently, I read in *Sailing Home* by Norman Fischer that the true self is behind and within, we feel it beneath the stories. The authentic self is there lurking, the true person of whom all the stories are told.

Perhaps, we are story itself.

# APPRECIATIONS TO

*"Gratitude is the memory of the heart."*
- Jean Baptiste Massieu, from Letter to Abbe Sicard

**Larry** – Your love sustains me.

**Jeff, Whitney, Brooke** – You teach me.

**Miriana, Todd, Phil** – We are family.

**Austin, Logan** – You inspire me to remember with wonder.

**Mother** – You birthed me. You taught me. You abide with me. I say thanks for you.

**Daddy** – Because you loved and affirmed me, with a promise to tell your story now.

**Bobby** – We share the same mother. Thank you for talking and listening.

**Nan, Molly, Charles** – Thanks for helping me remember.

**Uncle Curtis and Aunt Sis** – Thanks for the way you loved my mother and me.

**Uncle Howard and Aunt Dot** – Much appreciation for providing a place in our family's homeland, close to Mother's nursing home, to do this work of evoking memories.

**The Nursing Home and Hospice Caregivers** – Gratitude for the care you give everyday. **Kubena Funeral Home** – Appreciation for the dignity and respect you offer to the body of the deceased and to their grieving families.

**Don Anderson** – Because you are always there with your wisdom.

**Wayne Johnson** – Your coaching, mentoring, teaching, and editing made this book "lean forward." Gratitude to you for sharing your immense knowledge and skill.

**Jane Von Mehren** – Thanks for the publishing class and answering my e-mails.

**Susan Negley** – You are guide, goddess, guardian.

**Greg Martin and the Master Memoir Class in Taos** – Thanks for the feedback circle.

**Memoir In Twelve Chapters Class** – Bruce, Clay, Shirley, Sue, thank you for accepting my invitation and committing to a year long memoir writing experience together.

**Claire & David** – You are family. Thank you for giving me a second son.

**Pam & Jim** – Larry and I both value the spiritual explorations we engaged in with you.

**Mary Locke, Linda, Sylvia** – Our shared newsletter was a writing group in the mail. and our shared "growing up" culture was a safety net on the road to discovery.

**Sue, Muriel, Vivian** – Our retreats inspire and expand my thinking. We are "women who run with the wolves". You make it safe to disagree without distress.

**Texas Star Learners** – Together we explore books and different strategies for learning and teaching and my life and work continues to be enriched.

**Colorado Sixth Discipline** – Remember our goddess retreat? Thanks for taking the journey and for anointing goddesses with rose petals.

**Sacred Service Circle** – We explored the heart, opened it wider, listened to the silence, came closer to the Divine.

**JELM Writing Group & PUB Writing Group** – Thanks to those who gather to write and read and critique and encourage.

**Laughing Gull & Art Center for the Islands** – Appreciation for fostering the art of writing. A special thanks to **Ruth Asher** for her leadership in our writing community.

**Lucia** - your technical and teaching skills moved me forward.

**Natalie Goldberg** – *Writing Down the Bones*, and a week at your writing workshop in Taos, quieted my censor. **Taos Sevens** – Thanks for listening without judgment.

**Elizabeth Gilbert** – *Eat, Pray, Love* revealed to me the importance of structure and gave me permission to write from the gut.

**Mary Karr** – Your writing is courageous. I aspire to that kind of literary courage.

**Sylvia Plath** –You helped me to know my mother and, for that, I am eternally grateful.

**The Forum at Lincoln Heights Memoir Writing Group** – We just celebrated ten years of writing and reading our stories together. Your stories bless me.

## THANKS TO THE GODDESSES WHO ACCEPTED A PIECE OF MY MOTHER'S JEWELRY OR ONE OF HER SCARVES

Whitney
Brooke
Miriana
Nan
Molly
Cheryl Beth
Tina
Felecia
Ard
Judy
Claire

Mary Locke
Sylvia
Linda H..
Vivian
Sue
Muriel
Pam S.
Gwen
Lucia
Linda O.
Shirley H.

Mary Jane
Jayne
Susan
Margo
Barbara G.
Connie
Laurie
Rheagan
Roslyn
Betty
Kathleen

## AND TO THOSE GODDESSES IN MY PAST AND PRESENT WHO DEMONSTRATE/D ALL THE WAYS TO BE A WOMAN IN THIS WORLD –

Grandma Strode
Aunt Sis
Aunt Dot
Sissy
Aunt Benelle
Ruth P.
Gete
Lucy
Barbara M.
Azalea

Naomi
Patty
Lucille
Barbara Jo
Aunt Kate
Miss Annie
Mrs. Anderson
Mrs. Nelson
Jerry
Lydia C.

Merry F.
Dorothy P.
Martha G.
Ann Mc
Claire
Evelyn
Cheryl
Aunt Bell
Nancy Kay
Jane G.

*"those we meet for only one crucial moment, gaze to gaze, or for years know and don't recognize/ but of whom later a word sings back to us/ as if from high among leaves,/ still near but beyond sight/ drawing us from tree to tree/ towards the time and the unknown place/ where we shall know/ what it is to arrive."*
- Denise Levertov, From her poem, *I learned that her name was Proverb.*

# BOOKS THAT GUIDED ME ON THE JOURNEY OF DISCOVERING MY MOTHER WAS A GODDESS

*"I suggest that the only books that influence us are those for which we are ready, and which have gone a little farther down our particular path than we have yet got ourselves.*
- E.M. Forster, from *Two Cheers for Democracy*

Abernethy, Bob and Bole, William. *The Life of Meaning – Reflections on Faith, Doubt, and Repairing the World*. New York: Seven Stories Press, 2007.

Alzheimer's Association & Janssen Pharmaceutica Products, L.P. *Finding the Answers – A Resource Guide for Caretakers*. USA: Ortho-McNeil, 2002.

Anderson, Sherry P. and Patricia Hopkins. *The Feminine Face of God*. New York: Bantam, 1991.

Bolen, Jean Shinoda, *Goddesses in Everywoman*. San Francisco: Harper & Row, 1984.

Bolen, Jean Shinoda, *Goddesses in Older Women*. New York: HarperCollins, 2001.

Bridges, William. *The Way of Transition*. DeCapo Press, 2001.

Buechner, Frederick. *The Sacred Journey – A Memoir of Early Days*. San Francisco: HarperSanFrancisco, 1982.

Conforti, Michael. *Field, Form, and Fate – Patterns in Mind, Nature, and Psyche*. Woodstock, CT: Spring Publications, Inc., 1999.

Craighead, Meinrad. *The Mother's Songs*. New York: Paulist Press, 1986.

Doka, Kenneth J., Ed. *Living With Grief – Alzheimer's Disease*. Washington, D.C.: Hospice Foundation of America, 2004.

Estes, Clarissa Pinkola Estes. *Women Who Run With the Wolves*. New York: Ballantine Books, 1992.

Exley, Helen. *In Celebration of Women*. New York: Exley Publications, 1996.

Friday, Nancy. *My Mother/My Self*. New York: Delacorte Press. 1977.

Gibson, Clare. *Goddess Symbols*. New York: Barnes & Noble Books, 1998.

Hamilton, Edith. *Mythology*. New York: New American Library, 1942. [1940].

Hillman, James, *The Soul's Code*. Random House, 1996.

Johnson, Robert A. *Inner Work: Using Dreams and Active Imagination for Personal Growth*. New York: Harper & Row, 1986.

Johnson, Robert A. *Femininity Lost and Regained*. New York: Harper & Row, 1990.

Johnson, Robert A. *She*. Harper Paperbacks, revised edition, 1989.

Jung, C.G. *Aspects of the Feminine*. Princeton, N.J.: Princeton/Bollingen, 1982.

Kidd, Sue Monk. *The Secret Life of Bees*. Penguin (Non-classic), 2003.

King James Version, *The Holy Bible*. New York. The World Publishing Company.

Kubler-Ross, Elisabeth. *On Death and Dying*. New York: Macmillan, 1970.

Levine, Stephen. *Who Dies?* New York: Doubleday, 1982.

Luke, Helen M. *Such Stuff As Dreams Are Made On*. New York: Bell Tower, 2000.

Moore, Thomas. *Care of the Soul*. Harper Perennial, reprint edition, 1994.

Moore, Thomas. *Dark Nights of the Soul – A Guide To Finding Your Way Through Life's Ordeals*. New York: Gotham Books, 2004.

Moore, Thomas. *Original Self.* New York: HarperCollins, 2000.

Murdock, Maureen. *The Heroine's Journey.* Boston: Shambhala Publications, Inc., 1990.

Myss, Caroline. *Sacred Contracts – Awakening Your Divine Potential.* New York: Harmony Books, 2001.

O'Donohue, John. *Anam Cara.* Harper Collins, 1998.

O'Donohue. John. *Eternal Echoes.* Harper Perennial, 2000.

Oliver, Mary. *Long Life.* DeCapo Press, 2004.

Palmer, Parker J. *A Hidden Wholeness.* San Francisco: Jossey-Bass Inc., 2004.

Palmer, Parker J. *Let Your Life Speak.* San Francisco: Jossey-Bass Inc., 2000.

Plath, Sylvia. *The Bell Jar.* Harper Collins, 1996.

Plath, Sylvia. *The Unabridged Journals.* Anchor, 2000.

Raff, Jeffrey. *The Practice of Ally Work.* Berwick, Maine. Nicolas-Hays, Inc., 2006.

Sardello, Robert. *Silence.* Goldenstone Press, 2006.

Sardello, Robert. *The Power of Soul: Living the Twelve Virtues.* Hampton Roads Publishing, 2003.

Sewell, Marilyn, Ed. *Cries of the Spirit.* Boston: Beacon Press, 1991.

Small, Jacquelyn. *Psyche's Seeds.* Jeremy P. Tarcher/Putnam, 2001.

Stassinopoulos, Agapi. *Conversations with the Goddesses.* New York: Stewart, Tabori & Chang, 1999.

Rumi - "This Being Human Is A Guest House" from *The Essential Rumi* by Coleman Barks. HarperOne, 1997.

Walker, Alice. *The Color Purple*. Pocket, 1990.

Williamson, Marianne. *A Woman's Worth*. New York: Random House, 1992.

Woodman, Marion. *Conscious Femininity: Interviews with Marion Woodman*. Inner City Books, 1993.

Woodman, Marion with Mellick, Jill. *Coming Home to Myself*. Berkeley: Conari Press, 1998.

Woolger, Jennifer Barker and Woolger, Roger J. *The Goddess Within*. New York: Random House, 1987.

*"Some books are to be tasted, others to be swallowed, and some few to be chewed and digested."*
- *Francis Bacon, from Essays*

## MANY THANKS TO THE AUTHORS OF THESE WRITINGS FOR CREATING SOMETHING TO "BE CHEWED AND DIGESTED."

# GODDESS GLOSSARY

*"tell our daughters they are fragile as a bird*
*strong as a rose*
*deep as a word*
*and let them make their own growing*
*time big with tenderness."*
- Besmilr Brigham, From her poem *"tell our daughters"*

# GODDESS GLOSSARY

## ARTEMIS - GODDESS OF WILDLIFE AND INDEPENDENT SPIRIT

In the myth, Artemis was the daughter of Zeus and Leto, the firstborn twin sister of Apollo, god of the sun. As soon as Artemis was born, she both witnessed and midwifed her mother, Leto's, difficult labor to deliver Apollo.

As an archetype, Artemis personifies an independent feminine spirit that empowers a woman to pursue her own goals. She represents the concept of sisterhood – coming to the aid of her mother, protecting young girls and young wildlife, and acting in the role of big sister to her nymph companions. Artemis has an intense love of freedom, and is offended by the patriarchy's refusal to recognize her unique gifts as a woman.

Artemis is concerned with equality, justice, and fairness for people and animals. Motivated by these values, she may become an activist, and in her advocacy, she can be merciless. The pioneer woman shared the rugged, earth-woman qualities of this goddess, and understood what it was to live close to death and violence.

Humility is one of her teachers. Because of Artemis' strong feelings and lofty principles, she can be righteous and intolerant. However, she is capable of reflection and of feeling remorse as intense as her outrage.

## HESTIA – GODDESS OF HOME AND HEARTH AND TEMPLE

In the myth, Hestia was the first child born to Rhea and Cronus, the Titan parents of the first-generation Olympians. By birthright, she was one of the twelve major Olympians, yet she could not be found on

171

Mount Olympus because she was replaced by Dionysus. She was the only divinity of classical Greek mythology without a persona, no image, pose, art, or erotic pairing that make up Greek mythology.

As an archetype, Hestia represents an invisible feminine presence or energy that permeates a situation, a place, or a psyche, and transforms it into a sacred space. Hestia's hearth fire is about soul and home. Each household had a hearth, and each city had a common hearth in the main hall or temple. When people set out to start a new colony, they took the sacred fire from the mother fire to the daughter fires throughout the settled world. Hestia linked the old home with the new, the capital city with its colonies.

Unlike other Greed gods and goddesses, Hestia was not honored by storytellers or artists, she was honored in sacred rituals where she was the sacred fire. For thousands of years, fire was the only light in the dark, the only way to cook food, the only source of heat, a way to keep wild animals away and people together – home and hearth-fire were inseparable.

Hestia represented the serious responsibility of tending the fire and keeping the fire alive. This was a sacred act and one on which the survival of the group depended.

## APHRODITE – GODDESS OF SENSUALITY, LOVE, BEAUTY, AND SEXUALITY

In the myth, Aphrodite is born of the foam – a new birth out of water. Earth Mother, Gaia's, son, Kronos, threw the severed genitals of the Sky Father, Ouranos into the ocean. Kronos, god of agriculture, comes to render the tyranny of the sky, the mental realm, impotent. In this cosmic drama of earth, air, and water, he actually brings his tyrannical father not just down to earth, but down to water. In symbology, water often represents feeling and connection to the language of myth and dream.

As an archetype, Aphrodite represents patriarchy's inability to control the expansive nature of feminine energy. In the ancient world, a woman who could be both a sexual and spiritual confidante to a man was called the the Greeks a *hetaera*, literally a *companion*. The function of the *hetaira* is to awaken the individual psychic life in the male and lead him through and beyond his male responsibilities towards the formation of a total person.

Aphrodite was adored as the goddess of love, and her beautiful, divine son, Eros, was the embodiment of her greatest gift to mankind. Carl Jung defined eros in its more human context as relatedness, the quality of being connected. This gives us another clue to Aphrodite. As important as sexuality is to her, it is always part of being in relationship, and never an end in itself.

Relatedness is central to understanding Aphrodite. She wants us to be fully, feelingly, humanly present – related. Without that, she loses interest

## ATHENA – GODDESS OF WISDOM, CRAFTS, DISCERNMENT, LEADERSHIP

In the myth, Zeus himself gave birth to Athena from his holy head. She sprang forth from his head, waving her sharp spear. Olympus shook at the power of this bright-eyed goddess and the earth groaned, and the dark waves boiled and bubbled.

As an archetype, Athena represents the autonomously thinking feminine. Athena is very visible because she is extroverted, practical, and intelligent. Her fighting spirit enables her to be on the cutting edge of new ventures. She is tireless, courageous, loyal, persevering, single-minded, successful, and achieving.

Popular stories of Athena's restless masculine energy and of her being birthed by her father were explored as a political effort to incorporate an older, dispersed matriarchal tradition into the emerging but unstable patriarchy of early Athenians.

Athena is the rescuer from danger, the advisor for tight spots, the maintainer of life and health, and the wise leader of community gatherings. She symbolizes the inspiration for intellectual and spiritual productivity.

## DEMETER – GODDESS OF MOTHERHOOD, FERTILITY, AND HARVEST

In the myth, Demeter was the preeminent Mother Goddess and had the specialized duty of overseeing all forms of reproduction and renewal of life. Her central symbol was the sheaf of wheat. The heart of Demeter's myth centered around her loss, mourning, and reunion with her beloved daughter, Kore, whose name in Greek means maiden. Nearly all the stones and vase paintings show these two women together. This closeness of mother and daughter emphasizes how profoundly feminine this religious and mythological formation is. Kore, the daughter, later became known as Persephone.

An an archetype, Demeter represents the Great Goddess as triple – seen in the waxing moon, the full moon, and the waning moon, and in how she ruled the upper world, the earth, and the underworld. In human terms, she was Maiden, Mother, and Crone. It is these phases of a woman's life that are contained in Demeters's story. She sees herself as an innocent and untouched Maiden in her daughter, Kore/Persephone. She is Mother of that daughter and all that grows. When she loses her daughter, she plays the old woman, the Crone, whose childbearing years are gone, and who stands closer to death.

Much of the antagonism between contemporary mothers and daughters occurs when the mother sees in her daughter everything she never had and her love turns to bitterness and envy. She no longer sees herself in the innocence, purity, and beauty of this feminine being.

It is difficult for us today to imagine what it must have been like to have a goddess at the center of cultural and spiritual life. More than two thousand years of Judeo-Christian culture have influenced us in thinking of everything divine as masculine, occupying the heavens. We have almost forgotten what it is to honor the earth we walk upon as sacred, as our mother, and as the dwelling place of both goddesses and gods.

## PERSEPHONE – GODDESS OF DEATH, RENEWAL, AND TRANSFORMATION

In the myth, the goddess, Demeter, and her daughter, Persephone, were out in a field. Persephone was playing with the daughters of Ocean, away from Demeter. She was gathering flowers when she plucked a narcissus, a trap planted by Gaia for Zeus as a favor to Hades. The earth split wide open and the Lord of Death, Hades, appeared in his chariot and carried Persephone to the underworld to become his bride. She cried out, unheard.

As an archetype, Persephone represents the need for time alone to pursue secret projects, musings, and communions with the invisible world. Toni Wolff, Jung's close collaborator, said, "she must for instance express or act what 'is in the air,' what the environment cannot or will not admit, but what is a part of it…She is susceptible to being overwhelmed when contents, which traditionally would be called 'spirits,' flood her from…her unconscious mind. She needs a language for this." The door into Persephone's realm depression, withdrawal, suicidal fantasies – can be opened after a painful divorce, an unwanted move, an abortion, the loss of a job, surviving a serious accident, or any trauma. Always there is some kind of psychic, if not physical death.

Persephone's real issue is power, power that she refuses to own, forever gives away to successful or witchy women, influential men, or alcoholics. She fears Hades and the Dark Mother, who is none other than the powerful queen of the underworld she will not own in herself. She is still crying out for all-powerful Daddy Zeus to rescue her, and to her longed-for Mother Demeter to restore the comfort and innocence of her lost and forlorn childhood.

Persephone's deepest challenge is to unite the dark and the light sides of the goddess in herself.

## HERA – GODDESS OF MARRIAGE AND COMMITMENT AND PARTNER IN POWER

In the myth, Greeks proclaimed Hera as queen of the gods, who, with her husband, Zeus, ruled on Mount Olympus. In Homer's Iliad, she is depicted as a jealous and interfering wife. She had good reason to be jealous of Zeus because most of his offspring were conceived outside his marriage. The only god born from the marriage of Hera and Zeus was Ares, the god of war. Zeus and his promiscuity are an assertion of the power the Greeks placed in the fatherworld and the patriarchy. Hera's miserable marriage to Zeus was a portrait of the difficult uniting of the invading patriarchal warrior tribes with the existing matriarchal cults of the mother goddess, and also as a mirror of the stresses within the early Greek marital relationships.

As an archetype, Hera wants two things from her husband – partnership and equality. This means she wants as much power as he has. Throughout her life, a Hera woman is drawn toward power, position, and authority, particularly in politics, business, and the more patrician levels of society. She feels important giving her spouse input on meetings, deals, or crises he is negotiating.

Hera is perceived by Athena and Artemis as giving away all her power to her mate. But to Hera, she sees herself becoming more than she was as a single woman when she enters the marriage partnership. In her new role as wife and helpmate, she makes her husband complete and in return is the embodiment of his completion. Marriage can be seen as self-completion through the other, but how this occurs remains a mystery.

Hera wants to be out in the world where the action is. She doesn't want to live and work alone. The role of wife has deep meaning for her.

## MARY – MOTHER OF GOD, COMPASSION, HER NAME IS KINDNESS

In the Christian story, Mary, an unmarried virgin, is impregnated by God. She marries Joseph, a carpenter, and gives birth to the baby Jesus, the Savior, in a barn. The king of the country is threatened by the stories that Jesus is the king of the Jews and wants this baby murdered. Mary and Joseph flee to protect this child of God that has been entrusted to their care. At age twelve, Jesus tells his mother he must be about His Father's business, thus, separating Himself from her. She loves Him and, just as she'd held the space in her womb for Him, she held the space for Him to be loved by her in His absence.. She walks with Him to His crucifixion, bearing witness to His suffering, and loving Him every step of the way.

As a reminder of who we are as human beings, Mary shows us what it means to be dislocated from the very earth itself. Her Christian title, Queen of Heaven, shows her divine nature was thought of as spiritual in a heavenly way instead of in an earthly sense. Whatever connections Mary had to the earth were relegated to the heavens. As a result, it is hard for us to value the embodiment of the soul that Mary represents as much as we value the Holy Spirit, God unseen, in the heavens above.

Mary is about substance. She shows us that what we perceive and feels really matters. She teaches us that compassion is spiritual and psychological and, like all human gifts to do with our genetics and our environmental nurturing, can be easier for some than others. She reminds us that in cultures with an emphasis on hierarchy, war, greed, power, and domination, compassion can be perceived as weakness. She is viewed as unburdened by the need to be vindictive, castigating, or haughty.

Mary shows us that children must experience justice and love, be taught that they matter, and see empathy and compassion modeled in their families and their culture. That is love.

NOTE: Please see Book List on pp. 165-168 for more information on the goddesses.

# ABOUT THE AUTHOR

## BEVERLY CHARLES

*"…she also goes back to reflect on how intimate wounds
and fateful events have been part of her becoming.
One is reminded that Dante places in the Earthly
Paradise, at the top of the Mountain of Purgatory,
two rivers that must be crossed: first, Lethe, of ancient
heritage, in which the injuries, injustices, and passions
of the past must be forgotten or surrendered,
and second, Eunoe, Dante's own invention,
in which one must gather together,
remember, in the river of 'good mind,'
all that comes from one's past
and has contributed to who one essentially is."*
- Helen Luke, From *Such Stuff As Dreams Are Made On*

Beverly Charles is a learner, personally and professionally. After a career that included public and private school teaching and church ministry, she started her own consulting business, CONNECT. She developed and marketed a community building process and a leadership development course to public and private sector organizations here and abroad, served two terms on her local city council, and she currently serves as a leadership development coach to individuals. Being a mother (sometimes a single one) to three children while pursuing a career that would support her family and nurture her own vocational calling, she discovered she had been searching for the meaning of life and her place as a woman in this life since she was a child. Writing has been a part of Beverly's life since she began keeping a diary at age eight. She began teaching memoir workshops ten years ago and continues to enjoy facilitating memoir retreats where people tell and write their stories. She is an avid reader. Her interest in spiritual psychology and writing led her to attend workshops and retreats to deepen her understanding and broaden her knowledge. She lives with her husband, Larry Charles, in rural Texas. This is Beverly's first book. She is now working on a second book with one of her daughters. She can be reached at connectwbc@ cvctx.com.

### *"By the work one knows the workman."*
- Jean De La Fontaine

# MEMOIR WRITING WORKSHOPS

## AND

## HOW I DISCOVERED MY MOTHER IS A GODDESS WORKSHOPS

*Beverly Charles offers workshops on Memoir and Mystery and How I Discovered My Mother Is a Goddess. For further information about her work, please contact her at:*

BEVERLY CHARLES
P.O. Box 53
Oakland, TX 78951
979-562-2809 or 361-727-7035
E-mail: connectwbc@cvctx.com

A portion of the author's proceeds go to fund a scholarship in memory of her mother. The ECSB Scholarship will be given to a student majoring in early childhood education or special education or elementary education.

A portion of the author's proceeds go to
Alzheimer's Association
www.alz.org
P.O. Box 96011
Washington, DC  20090-6011
877-474-8259